Power Without Property

A NEW DEVELOPMENT IN AMERICAN POLITICAL ECONOMY

ADOLF A. BERLE, JR. *POWER WITHOUT PROPERTY*

A NEW DEVELOPMENT IN

AMERICAN POLITICAL ECONOMY

A Harvest Book
Harcourt, Brace & World, Inc. New York

Contents

Foreword

Princeton University complimented me by its invitation to deliver the Stafford Little Lectures there in the spring of 1958. This afforded opportunity to put together certain studies which have occupied me for some time. They raise the question whether, at least in the field of industrial evolution, the American system must now be examined from the point of view of political science as well as from that of economics.

While I was working at this, several interesting books appeared. One of them, Joseph A. Livingston's *The American Stockholder*, is referred to later. Another, a study of pension trusts by Dr. Paul Harbrecht, will shortly be brought out by The Twentieth Century Fund. I have seen it in manuscript and, with Dr. Harbrecht's permission, have used some of its figures. A third, Professor John Kenneth Galbraith's shattering book *The Affluent Society*, suggested new dimensions of economic thinking while I was revising the text. Mention also must be made of Dean Edward S. Mason's *Economic Concentration and the Monopoly Problem*. His point is not that the data as to concentration of power is necessarily wrong, but that

At least a part of the present emphasis on concentration arises, in all probability, from the illusion that at some not too remote period the economy was competitive.

Obviously a problem is not disposed of by saying that it always existed but merely was unrecognized.

At all events, the outline of a democratic economy does emerge as that of concentrated economic power, checked by and responsible to a "public consensus." This sets up a nice balance between the forces which may be called "democratic," and those whose authority is derived from historical property rights rather than from a popular mandate.

My thanks are due to the Seminar in Advanced Corporate Problems at Columbia University, three or four generations of which have debated some of these problems with me; to Dr. Paul Harbrecht for permission to use the material he had gathered; and to Dr. Max Ascoli for criticism of some theories of mine in the political science field.

I am likewise indebted to Miss Margaret Poole for attempting to reduce the manuscript to printable form.

Adolf A. Berle, Jr.

Columbia University,
January 1959

INTRODUCTION: *Four Prefaces,*
Respectively for Businessmen,
for American Liberals,
for Scholars, and for
the Uncommitted Public

I do not claim that the conclusions set out in this volume are certainties. Further study and criticism will modify them or perhaps overturn them altogether. I am convinced that anyone who has really faced the data presented and interpreted here will find that his idea of the processes and system we call "capitalist" will be permanently changed. This is a study of one series of connected economic chain reactions forming part of the continuing American social revolution. The revolution, energized by the driving forces which give it motion, powerfully affects the lives of all of us. It is likely to do so more visibly and more profoundly in years to come. Its processes are of particular interest to several groups presently involved in them, but they ought to be understood by everyone else. I therefore feel justified in writing a direct comment addressed to some of the groups whose interest has been engaged and whose opposition, in some instances, has been recorded.

Business and businessmen in recent decades have been the principal, though uncomprehending, instruments of this revolution. Liberals have been the chief mobilizers of periodic intervention in it by the political State. Scholars have provided the growing body of facts and, not less importantly, the apprehension of their significance through which we begin to understand the dynamics of this American movement. Obviously all of us are in this as participants, whether we know it or not.

Lifelong vibration between academic study of law and economics and a career not without turbulence at the bar, in business, and in foreign affairs and political office, has made it natural—almost instinctive—for me to feel a direct relation between the scholarly abstractions of political science and the social and political human results. I cannot think of big business without thinking of offices, and the men in them, or of economic policy without drawing mental pictures of men before investigating committees or bureaucrats operating their sets of regulations. Liberals and the liberal movement, a powerful and constant influence in American history, mean to me men I have known: my father, Louis D. Brandeis, Robert M. LaFollette, George Norris, Franklin Roosevelt, and my friends in politics and intellectual life who did the research, drafted the arguments, wrote the legislation, and fought the campaigns. Finally, it is, or at least should be, impossible for me or anyone else to consider an economic system apart from life's pulsing cinemascope of what happens to men, women, and especially children.

Yet the groups most involved show surprisingly little sign of awareness of their real part in this vast drama. Perhaps this is due to the fact that like most participants in political and social change, they commonly use the language of the past in considering the future. This is not because they are essentially backward-looking. It is rather because all language reflects past experience. The future and its idioms lie ahead. Only later do the new facts and new analyses command new descriptions.

In these four prefaces men are described as I think they are, rather than as they think they are. Some will be shocked. The businessman will find that he is a politician and a commissar—perhaps even a revolutionary one. The liberal finds himself a traditionalist. Both are encased in stereotypes which many will indignantly deny. The scholar finds himself at one and the same time a lord spiritual and a legislator.

The rest of us find ourselves involuntary voters in a fast and continuous election, continually changing a system of divided and competing property in the direction of a system of more or less controlled power. We may like it or dislike it· but we must understand it.

PREFACE FOR BUSINESSMEN

The American businessman, and especially the big business executive, at date of writing (1959) is in a singularly rough spot. Some know it; some do not. He has had at one and the same time a great deal less than his due, and a great deal more. Judged by net outturn results, American economy which is dominated now by big business has proved more productive than any in the world. Under the combined spur of social legislation and trades-union power, it has achieved a more or less continuous rise in standard of living—by which I mean real wages and purchasing power for almost everyone within the industrial system. Considerable progress has been made in eliminating the spasms of dishonesty or near dishonesty which too often disgraced our system in the past decades. Practically all the world, Communist as well as non-Communist, wants to duplicate this achievement.

True, the businessman had a great deal of help in doing this. Either in business or in government, any man who says "he" did something is generally a liar by the clock. He and a great many other people combined did it. Nevertheless the responsible heads of a system are entitled to take credit for success, just as they are invariably tarred with responsibility for failure. In other periods of history such men would have a measure of prestige and recognition accorded to few (if any) American businessmen. In the seventeenth century, they would have been made dukes. Even in half-socialist England today many have become hereditary peers, and those who really wish it wind up in the House of Lords. Since hereditary peerage means exclusion from the highest awards of British political life, a new method is award of life peerages, so that the accident of inheritance shall not exclude the business-man's son from entering Commons and shooting for a Cabinet post.

Not so in the United States. Few know, and most do not care, who are the current managers of General Electric or Aluminum Company of America, of United States Steel or American Telephone and Telegraph Company, of Allied Chemical or the Great Atlantic and Pacific Tea Company. In the publicly held corporations an American businessman ordinarily cannot honestly make a large fortune in the sense that Morgan, Vanderbilt, Belmont, Rockefeller, Mellon, and Davis made fortunes a generation ago. He can do quite nicely, make a comfortable stake, secure an excellent pension, and perhaps make a little on the side. With reasonable good fortune he can honestly become "little rich" and make comfortable provision for his family. But his son will have to go out and look for a job like anyone else unless, of course, he is content with the life of a moderately well-to-do loafer.

Businessmen can go into politics too, generally through the appointive route. Quite a number of them have recently held Cabinet posts in Washington. They rapidly discovered that there are more brickbats than halfpennies in this occupation. After tours of duty in which most of them have done their honest best, they were glad to return to a (relatively) sheltered life in Quaker Oats Company or in General Motors, in traditional big city banks or in business law firms. Generally they were greeted with questions like "Where have you been all this time?" when they returned. Only if they went into the business of peddling whatever political influence or friendships they might have (an unhappy tendency in my own profession) were they able to convert their experience to a solid, if somewhat questionable, financial asset. More often, avoiding political office, such men have tackled the job of doing something for the community. This might mean anything from raising an endowment fund for Alma Mater to establishing a foundation; but then the recognition and prestige they achieved was awarded not for their lasting economic and business achievements but for their extracurricular activity.

This, I think, is due to three causes.

First (about which nothing can be done) is that the United States keeps all its power-wielding personalities in order precisely by denying them permanent prestige—exceptions being made for a few outstanding men like Washington, Jackson, Lincoln, Wilson, and the two Roosevelts. (None of these were businessmen.) The European who thinks America is "materialist" might ponder this fact. Any American can tell him who Mark Twain was; few, if any, can remember who was Secretary of State at any time in history (present company, of course, excepted). One of the greatest we ever had, John Hay, is vastly better known because he wrote a life of Lincoln and a poem called "Little Breeches" than because he established peace in the Western Hemisphere through the Hay-Paunceforte Treaty. If men in politics fare as badly as this, how can one expect that the current businessmen will fare better?

The second reason is deeper. Businessmen have rarely accepted the necessity that a group or groups outside themselves shall appraise their work and pass judgment. By this I do not mean that they should be continuously subject to criticism; I mean that only a body of entirely independent opinion can effectively acclaim their achievements and condemn their failures. Businessmen are apt to take the view of the police-court defendant who was told he would get justice, and replied that this was what he was afraid of. Yet, obviously, only independent recognition is worth having. If you place enough advertising in the right places and your public relations staff does a moderately good job, you can receive an "award" (with plaque) from all kinds of organizations—from the Junior Chamber of Commerce in Port Lotus, Indiana, to the "Man of the Year" citation from the National Casketmakers Association or the Hi-Fidelity Station League. God forgive us all, you can even get honorary degrees from some universities, though by this I do not mean to denigrate the award an honorable college makes to an honorable businessman who has worked for it and has honorably deserved a "thank you" in the only way colleges can give it. Still and all, this lacks both charm and conviction. More often your recipient businessman will treasure most some tiny memento from a small and unpublicized group of independent associates who really did know the score, were so circumstanced that they did not have to say anything, but felt impelled to say quietly, sincerely, and independently that so-and-so had accomplished a notable job. But this is not community recognition and cannot take the place of it.

For this reason I have endeavored to state the need for a body of "Lords Spiritual" set over against "Lords Temporal," not merely as a need for the times, but also as a need for businessmen.

"Lords Spiritual" may seem an unfortunate phrase, but historically it is apposite. The feudal system was held to a degree of order (when it was) by the countervailing power (to quote Professor John Kenneth Galbraith's descriptive phrase) of the priests, the scholars, and divines comprehended within the body of the then universal Catholic Church. When that system worked well, the spiritual order erected generally accepted standards or criteria of judgment (in these studies represented rather than described by the symbol "public consensus"). It also determined, somewhat crudely but sufficiently, whether the holder of temporal power had measured up to these standards. This system was far from being foolproof; history has steadily to be called in to evaluate the mistakes and right the wrongs made and committed by the feudal Lords Spiritual. But, as far as I can see, some modern version of Lords Spiritual is the best we can do at the time.

At the moment, universities in America and their companion institutions of learning are the logical recipients of the mantle of the historical Lords Spiritual. This is one of the reasons (there are plenty of others) why you need them. It is also the reason why the minute you undermine their freedom, you lose the one quality you want most: the absolute independence of their judgment. When you receive an honorary citation from your own publicity department no one knows better than you that it is so much eye wash.

Now there is no reason at all why men who have pioneered, organized, or splendidly run a new source of supply, a communication system, a great operation of electronics, or the like, should not receive honors from universities or anyone else. But it would be refreshing if recognition could be had for real achievements: for having run that railroad for fifteen years extremely well; or for having (as has one big company) not only provided a good product but produced it with plants whose architecture commands admiration; or for other business achievements of like caliber. In other words, recognition ought to be for the real achievements rather than for the extracurricular ones.

The third difficulty lies in the fact that big businessmen are in politics, much as they hate to admit it. The fact is obvious. Since they are not owners but only managers, they really are a variety of non-Statist civil servant. Their direct responsibility is to four groups: the community from which their companies buy; the community to which their companies sell; the employees which their companies hire; the security holders to whom the companies pay interest and dividends. Add to these the peripheral contacts, and their constituencies are, actually, larger than those of most professing politicians. In aggregate this is a large body of public opinion. This public opinion from time to time invokes intervention of the formal political government, frequently through Congressional investigation. Voluntary or involuntary emergence on the stage of formal politics is always possible for any big businessman. For the heads of the very greatest concerns, indeed, this political role is practically continuous, though in varying degrees of stress. Handling this end of the modern management task is as much part of their job as dealing with personnel, plant construction, or price policy. But politics is always a matter of give-and-take. A shot from your side is answered by a volley from the other. There is little serenity and frequently not much dignity allowed in the process. Getting out of it with a whole skin is about the best you can do. American political life means that the politician mounts the public opinion bronco, rides it as long as he can, and is fortunate if in the end he is not bucked off. In result, American businessmen often close their business careers with less honor and credit than many of them deserve.

On the other hand, you get more than is coming to you in certain respects. The American public still naïvely assumes that a man successful at some things is wise in everything, just as in the old days the Chinese peasant assumed that anyone with a university education could cure a common cold or repair a watch. Transitory magazine and newspaper print gives remarkable publicity and attention to the expressed views of any prominent businessman. On one occasion, a quite successful manufacturer of elevators emerged as an authority on education of young girls. Henry Ford was lured into several side matters where publicity was great (and where he was obviously wrong). Embassies and other most delicate matters of government are frequently confided to businessmen, though the problems are anything but those comprehended within business experience.

This can be dangerous, because temptation is omnipresent and punishment for a fall is inevitable. It is arduous enough in all conscience to live up to a real reputation. Attempting to live up to a false or fraudulent one is literally hell on earth. None the less, the illusion that a successful businessman is all-wise or all-powerful is so easily created, and is so cheerfully accepted by so much of the American public, that at any given moment big businessmen find themselves in positions disproportionate or irrelevant to their real equipment.

All in all, I think, the big businessman is regularly offered more power than is justified by his business position. (He may, and often does, have other justification for the offer; that depends on how wide his nonbusiness thinking and experience may have been.) He would be more than human if he did not like the sensation. But he is less than intelligent when he takes it seriously. If a first-rate financier found himself holding a scalpel in a delicate brain operation with power of life and death over the patient, he would have brains enough to get out of the situation at once and put the scalpel into the hands of a competent surgeon. He may be under exactly the same obligation when asked to pass on the problem, say, of whether trade with Communist China will or will not forward the cause of peace, or whether extended social security will or will not benefit the American social system.

Both of these are no less delicate; either may be equally out of the field of his equipment. Nevertheless, businessmen are all too easily persuaded to move in and influence decision.

All this merely adds up to the proposition that businessmen are human. They have virtues and failings; they have strengths and weaknesses; their reactions are defensive like those of most people.

Some of us who study try to go through abstractions and deal with real situations. In every problem every projected solution at bottom has to answer two questions: Who goes where? What is he expected to do when he gets there? The statistical aggregates of economists and the summing-up of political scientists measure the results.

These studies attempt to discuss one aspect of the American economic system, not in terms of assumed motivations or philosophical morals, but rather in terms of what has happened in one sector and what apparently will happen if current tendencies continue. They may be disturbing because they call attention to situations which have existed relatively unnoticed. But the situations cannot be avoided by sweeping them under the rug, though the silent treatment might win a year or two of quiet—a brief span during which the American consensus will not go to work on them. Their magnitude is such that some development of public opinion is, I think, inevitable. I suggest it is far better to meet these matters while they can be dealt with as subjects for rational study and courteous debate, giving possibility of intelligent guidance, than to wait until there is an explosion like the explosion which half a century ago brought the Armstrong investigation in life insurance and the Pujo investigation into the so-called money trust.

The American economic system is getting away on a new base with a great many merits and some dangers. The time to study it and think about it and do whatever has to be done is in the next few years rather than later.

PREFACE FOR AMERICAN LIBERALS

Whenever American business, especially American big business, and American corporations are mentioned, your American liberal almost instinctively snaps his thinking into a stereotype. Big business is the "enemy." Its interests are opposed to "the people." You are on one side or the other. If recognition is paid to the solid achievements of big business, including the substantial advance it has made toward meeting a social point of view, you must have sold out to the enemy. If you whale away with charges, you ought to be supported by liberals quite irrespective of whether objective fact and cold reasoning support the accusations.

Historically, there is a good deal to be said for the stereotype. Nobody could have accused big business of innate humanity, or of interest in either the worker or the consumer, or even of awareness of the American community until about the fourth decade of the twentieth century. Most of the indictments leveled against railroads and against commodity monopolies by the Populist movement proved factual. Theodore Roosevelt's charge that some multimillionaires were "malefactors of great wealth" had solid basis. The methods used by big interests to stifle criticism or, more often, to break their critics were outrageous. The campaign of vicious personal attack leveled at Louis D. Brandeis when he fought the indefensible financial schemes of the New York, New Haven & Hartford Railroad from 1910 to 1916 was unusual only because it attracted attention and backfired. The brute force of propaganda, vilification, personal abuse, political intrigue, and whipped-up hatred against the Roosevelt reforms in the days of the New Deal is not easily forgotten by anyone who, like this writer, experienced it. Generally speaking, business indiscriminately attacked anyone of public importance who was not considered "business-minded." They did worse: they sought, though without great success, to prevent circulation even of factual studies calling attention to actual situations, lest these provoke deeper inquiry. Battle appeared to be perpetually joined. Since the business community took its positions instinctively and carried on its attacks with an emotional hatred in direct ratio to the bite of liberal criticism, it is hardly strange that liberals instinctively reacted in opposition.

European thinking to some extent entered the situation. There, more formal political warfare existed. Socialism, Marxian and otherwise, accepted the dogma of the "class war." Either you believed in the property system, or you believed in the "social" system; no alternative was allowed. In the form of Communist thinking, this hard-and-fast, black-and-white, heaven-or-hell division entered American thinking as it permeated European. Some American intellectuals fell for this intellectual line. The breakdown (it was quite simply that) of the American economic system in 1932-1933 mightily assisted.

Nevertheless, liberals were not only wrong in accepting this sharp division; they violated an essential law of their being in falling in with the stereotype. If liberalism means anything, it means adherence to two propositions. First, you get the facts and draw the conclusions objective survey of the facts requires. Second, you steer steadily for the greatest freedom and self-realization of individuals—which means that an economic system is judged by its content and results, not by its form. Concentration of economic power is a fact, and the dangers of power are clear. But along with it went distribution of property and even wider distribution of national income. The revolution in American economic life went almost unnoticed because liberals persisted in thinking of a publicly held corporation in much the same way that they had thought of individual monopolists like Jay Gould or Commodore Vanderbilt, though its results were quite different. Similarly, they thought of ownership by "the people" as something real, whereas a moment's thinking would make it clear that "the people" was an abstraction. Its reality meant some sort of bureaucratic management. No one ever met "the proletariat" or found out what he had for breakfast, but "dictatorship" of the proletariat proved as real and bloody and terrible as Josef Stalin. The tendency to look to an abstraction and ignore human beings is a vice which big business has frequently indulged. It is a vice not permitted to liberals who must deal with actual, not imaginary, facts.

Not all liberals yielded to the temptation. Fiorello H. La-Guardia was a political liberal if ever there was one; but no one recognized more solidly than he that big business probably was the best avenue toward providing decent conditions for labor. In conversation with the writer, he once flung out against liberal preoccupation with "little business," wondering whether any of them ever encountered the garment trades or small landlordism in New York. Any honest trades-union leader could have borne witness that achieving decent wages and decent conditions (let alone continuous employment) depended on having solvent and strong employers. This involved, among other things, an adequate size of operation. There is plenty of place for small business, and it has certain essential virtues just as there are plenty of dangers in big business. But it was absurd for liberals to swallow the fiction that all virtue lay in smallness, and that all vice inhered in size.

Opposition to size as such became a form of liberal stereotype. In these studies there is included later a discussion of what is sometimes called "the Brandeis School," the men who carry on Brandeis' famous battle against the curse of bigness. I knew Brandeis from my childhood. My first job was in his law office in Boston. I loved him to the day of his death. But I think were Brandeis in action today, he would be the first to deal with the facts and the last to fetter his view with fiction. At bottom Brandeis wanted honest and socially minded business. He disliked bigness because he considered, rightly, that the men creating and operating it did not understand what they were doing and, because they pretended to understand what they were doing, turned themselves into pious frauds. For that matter, he had a very similar worry about men in government. He was fond of telling the story of the successor to Ballinger who resigned as Taft's Secretary of Interior as a result of Brandeis' Ballinger-Pinchot investigation. The newly appointed Secretary asked Brandeis if he had any advice to offer. Brandeis replied, "Always understand the meaning of every paper you are asked to sign." The answer, unhappily accurate, was short: "Dear Brandeis: You ask the impossible."

Well, techniques, economics, and the growth of affairs have not given us littleness either in business or in government and apparently are not going to. We as liberals, of course, can roam the earth like Jeremiah, insisting that this is a naughty world which should be put together in a quite different fashion. This is all very well as an intellectual avocation. But it can conceal ignominious flight from the firing line. If we cannot have an economy primarily based on small business, the best thing we can do is to understand the business we do have, to know what results we want from it, and to do our best to assure that these results are produced. This means that we, or some of us, are tackling the dubious and ill-paid job of being Lords Spiritual, that is, keepers and developers of the public consensus. Sometimes we must come like the Prophet Elijah into the presence of Ahab, demanding redress for known wrongs. But at all times we should be watching what the system does, encouraging whatever rightness that comes out of it, and being quite fearless in seeking so to mold the course of events that as little wrong and as much right comes out of it as possible.

Finally, liberals have to recognize a solid fact. Business is, in the main, the economic service-of-supply of the United States. In some fields, possibly electric power for one example, government organisms can do better than private business, as the Tennessee Valley Authority and Columbia River projects have shown. But there is danger in merging political government with the economic system—perhaps as great as that inhering in concentrated economic power not tied up with the political system. Now a government cannot be perpetually at war with its service-of-supply. More accurately, it cannot maintain such a war on all fronts, for there will always be areas in which social interest conflicts with the interest of any economic pyramid, private or public. In those areas battles have to be fought out. But it is one thing to say that, and quite another to say that democratic government and politics must be in perpetual conflict with business and to assume that businessmen will always refuse to measure up to the obligations of economic statesmanship because of misplaced ambition or built-in lack of character.

The liberal task, at the moment, seems to me to be that of stating and making specific issues where specific issues should be made. I think it will be found that in most cases the issues will turn, less on the theoretical validity of a system, than on whether the administrators of particular enterprises are living up to the obligations of the system itself. It is one thing, for example, to accuse Anaconda Copper Company of doing things it should not in Montana. It would be quite another to assert that Anaconda Copper should not exist at all. It was one thing to assert that the public utility holding company pyramids of the 1920's violated most of the obligations of decent economics and many of the obligations of common honesty. It was quite another to say that the electric power business should be run by small units. It was one thing to say, truthfully, that public utility companies had refused to supply the rural consumers and had proved unable to develop the area served by the Tennessee Valley Authority. It proved quite wrong to draw the conclusion that all rural consumers had to be supplied by the government. It proved quite right to conclude that only a government operation could develop the Tennessee Valley. The precise difference between liberals and dogmatic Communists, Socialists, or old-style capitalists is that the liberal is driving for human results and not for the victory of any dogma.

The nondogmatic quality of American political economic action has been, I believe, one of the great (possibly the greatest) forces in giving to the United States the productivity it now enjoys. President Franklin Roosevelt once had a heated conference in the White House. Some of his Staff insisted that he was pursuing inconsistent systems in his policy of internal development. Afterward he said to me: "This country is big enough to experiment with several diverse systems and follow several different lines. Why must we put our economic policy in a single systemic strait jacket?" Of course, he was right. The social regeneration of the Tennessee Valley was one problem which probably could only be done by government. Getting electric wires to farms was another: it could be done either privately or through cooperatives, and actually was done by both methods. Nobody thinks of the St. Lawrence Canal or the toll road system as "Socialist" (though they certainly are just that), just as no one thinks of the American Telephone & Telegraph Company as a private monopoly. They are merely appropriate ways of getting things done—the best available ways, in fact, under present circumstances.

Liberals, I suggest, should be the observers, the fact-finders, and the critics, as free to praise as to condemn, as free to support as to attack. They are bound by their preoccupation with human beings to judge on the basis of present and foreseeable human results. This will give them, the Lord knows, enough work to do, enough adventures to essay, enough dangers to run. It will not in the slightest prevent them from thinking through their value systems, or from drawing architects' plans for the *Civitas Dei* they dream of creating.

PREFACE FOR SCHOLARS

Academic study of the working of any major part of the American economic system at its present stage must now, I submit, overpass the generally accepted limits of technical economics. Any thorough analysis indicates its intrusion into the American political system—or intrusion into it from the political side. The two systems are, and perhaps always were, interlocked. In any case, the two interact deeply and continuously. Unless some unforeseen change occurs, this interaction will become more profound. It is a fair question now whether sound academic distinction can be made between political science and economics. The breakdown of the economic unit we regarded as "property" into its component elements may be matter of economic analysis. But one outstanding result of it—the erection of organizations largely resting on and certainly developing power—plainly raises problems whose nature is essentially political.

Paucity of academic recognition of the ensuing situation is partly due to the severe limitation which many scholars have placed on their work. This is natural, but it is also dangerous. For example, you may study pension trusts or life insurance companies as more or less isolated phenomena. You can find out a great deal about their size, their coverage, the number of beneficiaries, and so forth, and stop there. Or you can study the concentration of industry in large corporations, the percentage of industry which any one of them or a group of them have, the amount of their assets, their cost of production, price policies, and so forth. Again, an interesting subject. Or you can study the process of formation of capital, how and where capital is accumulated, and the means by which it is gathered. Again, an interesting body of information. But when you hook up all three in series (which is what I have done in the following chapters), you begin to see the dim outlines of a tremendously significant political and social as well as economic force. Briefly, some five hundred great corporations dominate through outright ownership two-thirds of the industry of the United States. This is the present situation. But a study of the figures on capital formation develops the fact that these same corporations accumulate the greater part of three-fifths or 60 per cent of the capital which United States applies to industrial use. This is a powerful element of control of the economic and social future of the United States. Capacity to apply that capital is capacity to determine when, where, and how future American development will go on. Now put behind these two elements the growing size of pension trusts, mutual funds, and life insurance companies, and the growing propensity peculiar to pension trusts and mutual funds to buy up the stock of these same five hundred corporations. This accumulates in them the ancient right to vote for and choose managements—an historical survival of property power remaining from the smaller-enterprise days. Couple that with the fact that the pensioner or policyholder is completely separated in fact and almost equally separated in law from any connection with the corporation: pension trustees, mutual fund managers, or life insurance executives now perform the function previously held by the individual stockholder of choosing management. Past rights are collectivized; present capacity is concentrated; future development of economic government will be by relatively few men. These men are detached from the conventional workings of the profit system; they become, in fact, an unrecognized group of professional administrators distributing the fruits of the American industrial system, directing its present activities, and selecting the path of its future growth.

You may call this an industrial system, or, if you choose, a dominant sector of an economic system. You may call it a power system, or you may call it a non-Statist political system. All terms would be more or less accurately applied. Equally, you may call the result "Collectivism" or "non-Statist Social-ism" or "Peoples' Capitalism," depending on which character-istic interests you most. The merest glance at the growth of the system, not to mention its achievements, demonstrates the fact that, under whatever name, an institutionalized proc-ess is carrying an enormous current freight and is moving forward toward greater responsibility at (historically con-sidered) breakneck speed.

Invariably, having appreciated this, someone rises to at-tack the analysis because it leaves out the power of organized labor. The criticism is valid if the synthesis I have just de-scribed purported to be a complete picture of the American scene; otherwise it is stupid. Obviously labor is a force rapidly becoming, if not already, comparable to the force just de-scribed. If anything, power is more concentrated in the labor movement than it is on the capitalist side. Professor John Kenneth Galbraith of Harvard pointed that out in his *Ameri-can Capitalism: A System of Countervailing Power*, though I am not convinced that big labor unions emerged as a response to big corporations. My impression is that both concentra-tions emerged at about the same time, spontaneously. Prob-ably, if enough men were not bound to specialized studies of specialized sectors we should discover that there were other forces, perhaps comparable in thrust, whose existence we simply do not apprehend.

The Modern Corporation and Private Property, my first study, pointed out the concentration of wealth and power in large corporations. It seemed to me that it in no way broke new ground. For at least twenty years prior to that study, corporations and their bigness had been the subject of dis-cussion and controversy. I thought we were merely describing a phenomenon with which everyone was familiar, and still think so. But the phenomenon had not, apparently, received academic attention. My point is merely that we have yet to read a thoroughgoing attempt to describe and analyze as a whole the modern American system, though despite obvious defects it is the most productive and in its way the most remarkable large-scale economic system in modern history—perhaps in any history.

To criticize the study of one major current within this system because it does not also take up and analyze another major current is beside the point. Obviously many of the theoretical considerations which apply to big capital organizations will also apply to big labor organizations. But some of them will not. Aggregated money, machinery, and management are not the same as are men, their aggregated labor, and their centralized leadership. Also there are other elements. A third major force, for example, which no one knows much about is the massed economic power of the Pentagon and the American Armed Services: a force which did not exist in the American scene prior to 1940 and which as a peacetime force is a novelty in American life.

So I hope these essays will be taken for what they are: studies of one of the major forces (but not the only major force) which is steadily and almost unintentionally transforming American life—and doing this with less agony, less noise, less waste (yes, less waste in spite of a plethora of that) than seems to be the case in the other twentieth-century revolutions currently proceeding in most of the world.

Some economists have never quite decided whether they were evangelists preaching a true gospel, or reporters of current phenomena, or analysts and interpreters of data enabling men to make more reasoned choices. There is to be sure no reason why an economist should not be any one of these or, indeed, why he should not be several other things besides. There is, however, sound reason for asking him to call his shot. If he believes that desertion of the rule of *laissez faire* by a weak human race has committed a large part of America to mortal sin, destining it to eventual damnation, he has every right to say so. But, of course, he is then preaching a gospel and making propaganda for a world that does not exist (and never did), and it is only fair that he should acknowledge this. Again if he wishes to describe banks or the course of prices in commodity markets, without indicating whether the data has any use or what the use might be, he has a perfect right to do that. It is a wholly legitimate task. But he ought then to say that he is accumulating material which he hopes somebody else will use. If he has discerned a new method of discovering what goes on—for example, the inflow-outflow method of description—he can either stop there, or he can indicate where causes can be related to effects and what new deductions can be drawn from his data.

But when the economist's projections show that the forces he studies and measures have become involved with political processes, his interpretations must import data outside the scope normally considered "economic." The political scientist with all his deficiencies has at least steadily recognized this fact. He knows the political system invariably reflects something else: a value system, and the habits, culture, and institutions built around or because of it. The evangelist-economist, usually without recognizing it, subsumes *some* value judgments: this is why he wants a different system than what he has got, or hopes to correct the errors of our present wayward course. It is wholly unfair in any case to criticize an economist for recognizing the political elements in his system; rather he ought to be criticized if he does not recognize them. But he ought to be more or less explicit about it.

This is why, in these essays, there is a chapter on the theory of economic power. If you hook up in series the three trends we noted above and you discover that one resultant is economic power held in large measure by a few people, the point has little significance except in political terms. If you are a totalitarian, the more concentration of power the better; it does not matter what kinds of power are mixed together. If you are an individualist, you begin to think in terms of safeguards and wonder if there are any. Observing the American scene you note that, as power goes, the present concentration has in recent years been (on the whole) relatively free from the excesses which often make concentrated power odious. Certainly this was not because historical chance had located American economic power in a collection of saints. Checks (not "balances") appeared in the form of periodic political interventions demanded by American public opinion. To explain this it becomes necessary to import a political conception—the "public consensus"—familiar to the political scientists and brilliantly explained a few years ago by Mr. Walter Lippmann. So, it seems, the ultimate protection of individuals lies not in the play of economic forces in free markets, but in a set of value judgments so widely accepted and deeply held in the United States that public opinion can energize political action when needed to prevent power from violating these values.

The job has not in all respects been a good job. The remarkable thing (to paraphrase Dr. Samuel Johnson) is that the job gets done at all. Empirically we can only say that this consensus is adequate enough to give bounds to the current use of economic power by the capital-controlling organization. No one quite knows whether that same consensus could likewise check the power, say, of labor unions or of the Pentagon were either to get out of hand. In our field, we must squarely face the fact that economics and politics are now part of a central cumulus whose full description has not yet been attempted by anyone.

Eventually, I suppose, a man will rise (I think it will be

a man, not a committee) who thinks out and writes down a *schema* of the American system in which we live. Had we been a Latin country, say, France or Italy or Spain, someone would have attempted this long before. Your true continental simply cannot understand plowing along a road without a map, or collecting data without some theory of classification in arrangement. His fault is that he may attempt to describe a structure before he has the materials. Americans on their side rather resist attempting it at all even when plenty of material is handy. My impression is that enough material is available now to justify ambitious men in undertaking a classification.

Whether these men will hold Ph.D. trades union cards as economists, or as political scientists, or possibly even as sociologists is entirely immaterial. They are all, at base, working with the same body of data, and all are merely barging into that mass from different sides of it.

Finally, a difficulty must be noted. The American economic system is primarily a business system. Businessmen, by and large, suffer from split-personality. They know they are doing important things and have the normal human desire both to understand how important they are and to have other people understand them. They also have a clear realization that if this importance is realized, all kinds of people will develop an interest which may be definitely hostile to what they are doing and possibly to their being there at all. This leads to a strong desire to have the subject dropped—or at least to see that presentation is made by their own publicity departments or by men in whom they have "confidence." They are, in fact, at that perilous, agonizing point in history when they must emerge into the public light democratic politicians must endure. They can hardly be blamed if they shy at the prospect; they can be blamed if they do not accept the inevitable results of the positions they have reached. Academic students must recognize this and take their chances. Business opinion, after all, is only one (and not the most important) evaluation of the quality of their work.

PREFACE FOR THE UNCOMMITTED PUBLIC

As the American economic system continues its headlong development, each of us must recognize we are all in it. This realization ought to be in two brackets. The system does things to all of us. Equally, all of us do things to it. We are both benefactors and beneficiaries, oppressors and victims, framers of it and constrained by it.

Quantities of literature have appeared exciting concern for the downtrodden masses. But the American masses are not downtrodden. Justification for this literature did exist in the nineteenth and early twentieth centuries when Europe was emerging from the feudal system, when to be base-born meant to be deprived of participation, when the early phases of the capitalist system were doing to the public very much what Chinese Communism is doing to the Chinese public today. But in America that era is substantially over in all save a few unreconstructed pockets. There is little excuse for masses here to adopt a self-pitying attitude, while it is as a rule unvarnished demagogy for politicians, liberals, or scholars to pull out that stop. By comparative standards the men and women composing the American "public" are both individually and on an average better off than any substantial population block in history. Further, whenever they really want a change in their situation, they can get it. There are, of course, physical limits, but even these are steadily widening.

What you and I really want from the American economic system is very likely to be what you and I will receive. Our real difficulty is discovering exactly what we do wish, and our dilemma is that frequently we wish inconsistent things. One may dream of a peaceful bucolic life, only to find that having achieved it most of us also want shops, motion-picture theatres, and access to varied forms of life found only in cities. We may hope to be heads of enterprises which we own and control, only to discover that we do not wish the risks, the personal responsibilities, and the unrelieved strain which such a situation entails. We may even wish for a twenty-hour work week, and then discover that unoccupied time or a task which does not engage full interest makes not for happiness but for a sense of futility. In these dilemmas the dominant desire finally dictates choice. Most people do what they really want to do.

One result of all this is what we call "the economic system."

It so happens that the American public wanted and got a great many things whose production and distribution have caused the phenomenon of big business. They wanted forms of economic safety which required and brought into existence huge insurance companies, pension trusts, and similar financial institutions. They wanted the products of techniques which can only be developed at great expense, maintained on large scale, and operated by an experienced and trained elite. They wanted these things because they wanted a life offering security, comfort, variety, and flexibility. They got and are getting the social-economic institutions which satisfy these wants. These institutions become, and are, foci and bearers of power.

There is evidence that American wants go far deeper. This, the most prosperous population in the world, seems also affected by a widespread malaise. Prosperity, indeed, may be the precise cause of this restlessness. As material needs of life approach satisfaction, spiritual needs become more demanding. But problems of the spirit are neither defined nor met by our economic system. Probably they never can be; I think they never should be. Power is not an end, only a means to an end.

It will be found in these pages that the power system emerging in response to public wants is at long last governed by public consensus. In creating, maintaining, and expanding that consensus all of us have a part. It is a sort of continuing election in which there are no nonvoters. Any feeling however individual, any form of consumption however insignificant, any participation however humble exerts its effect. In economic as in political government, a people gets (more or less) the government it deserves. Certainly that is true in as sensitive and free a democracy as ours. Even our hopes for the future have formative influence. Professor George Herbert Palmer of Harvard used to make a deep and penetrating observation to his students: "Young gentlemen, be careful of your dreams. Dreams are dangerous things, apt to be fulfilled."

The power system we have, and call—or miscall—capitalism is the resultant of the American dreams of the past. Its future testing will be determined by American dreams of the civilization Americans hope to achieve. We shall control—or be controlled by—our power-bearers, as our desires and our choices determine.

The chain reaction of capital formation and aggregation of economic power explained in these essays shows (in one aspect) how the process works. What it will do depends on all of us.

1 *The Habits of Capital and Their Impact*

THE CHANGING PICTURE OF CAPITAL

We live under a system described in obsolete terms. We have come to believe our own repeated declarations that our society is based on individual initiative—whereas, in fact, most of it is no more individual than an infantry division. We assume that our economic system is based on "private property." Yet most industrial property is no more private than a seat in a subway train, and indeed it is questionable whether much of it can be called "property" at all. We indignantly deny that we are collectivist, yet it is demonstrable that more than two-thirds of our enterprise is possible only because it is collectivist: what is really meant is that the State did not do the collectivizing. We think of capital as the fruit of individual savings, whereas it really is the result of various methods of compulsion. Further, all capital is not alike.

These are sweeping statements and should not be accepted without supporting data. This chapter is intended to give their statistical base.

Because our system is commonly called "capitalist," we begin by considering the habits of capital. Particularly we are interested in the impact of some of its habits upon the structure of American political economy. "Capital" is here used in the superficial sense commonly employed in business and finance: the money devoted to more or less permanent investment in productive enterprise. We shall discover that even this limited use requires subdivision, when capital is regarded from the point of view of its assumed owners. One block of this money, at time of accumulation or investment, is assumed to be "risk capital" involving relatively high degree of loss danger. Another block is more or less dedicated to investment without risk; at least the risk is minimized. It will presently appear that determination whether capital is to be with risk or without risk (minimal risk) is primarily made, somewhat surprisingly, not at time of investment but in process of accumulation. The odd fact is that a so-called "capitalist" system evidenced surprisingly little interest in capital until relatively recently.

Classical economists had told us, accurately, that "capital" was the fruit of saving. Developing this idea, saving was considered to be a cutting down of consumption below production and devotion of the balance to permanent plant. Nothing was simpler than to draw the picture of an individual earning more money than he spent and investing his money savings. These, aggregated, added up to capital. The simple picture then developed complexities. Savings could be enforced upon our type-individual. For example, the government might tax him and use part of the taxes to construct permanent capital improvements. This is sometimes described as "forced savings." Again, no line has really been drawn between "consumption" and productive expenditure. The workman's house is his shelter and his home; he enjoys it and consumes it gradually; his automobile is an enjoyable adjunct to his life and he "consumes" that. But without house and transport, no labor force would be available to run any plant in the United States. Provision for this type of consumption is, therefore (at least partly), required capital expenditure as any enterpriser who has ever built a plant in empty country thoroughly understands. The assumed "clear" lines of traditional thinking at once become unclear. Again, it was assumed that "labor" could be separated from capital. So, of course, in a human sense it could; but the fact was that if labor could be conscripted as ancient Egyptians and modern Russians and Chinese have done, the product of that labor (over and above subsistence for the men involved) could presently take form as permanent addition to plant in the form of a pyramid, a port, or a power-plant dam. Again this was a type of "forced savings." But the word has shifted its bearing and its sights; measurements were wanting. Most analysts were content to leave the conception of "savings" and resulting capital in an ideological limbo.

The financier and the enterpriser, the banker and the corporation, of course, could not. The latter had to have money with which to organize, construct, develop, and enlarge the production facilities of their enterprises; the former had to assist in finding it. To both, the problem resolved itself into money. This, at least, was measurable; though it is less than forty years ago that serious figures on the subject began to be collected in the United States. The Department of Commerce set up figures in 1919 and has continued them ever since, though the base was somewhat changed in 1929. The ensuing figures can only be considered a crude guess, at least up to 1947. They do, however, give an approximate map of what happened, though later cartographers will eventually give us a truer picture. Probably the map bears about the same relation to the reality that a late fifteenth-century explorer's map of North America bears to current cartography. The general outlines nevertheless are useful.

They are also surprising. They show, among other things, the inadequacy of the word "savings," chiefly because the "saver" somehow seems to vanish from the picture. As we shall see, he is steadily retreating into the background of economic history. As he retreats, our real subject of interest—a new form of economic institution—moves into the foreground, quietly effecting a revolution already half accomplished and apparently headed for more drastic accomplishments in the coming decade.

Some tentative measurements in the form of scratch-figures were privately made ten years ago. More recently, government figures give a fair picture of the course of capital development. Let us look at the picture.

CAPITAL: 1919–1947

Here we are dealing with monetary measure of "capital." In this respect "capital" is arbitrarily defined. We already noted that the precise difference between consumption and productive capital was anything but clear, and that devotion of labor toward a capital result was just as valid an element of capital formation as savings measurable in money. The only consumption figure here included is housing; the only labor measurement is concealed in money, a substantial part of which went to wages. The result is, therefore, an approximation.

The Location of Savings

Though investment of risk capital is an absolute essential of the functioning of the capitalist system, there is surprisingly little accurate information on the source from which risk capital can be expected, or the degree of flow.

Our search here is not for theoretical "savings," but for actual cash which can be made available for venture capital by some process. This means, substantially, that we are seeking a picture, not of national savings as an economic abstraction, but of the savings of actual individuals or corporations, available in cash, and not so committed in advance that they cannot be channeled into new ventures. The composite picture

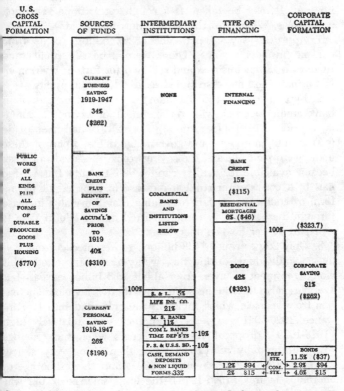

U. S. CAPITAL MARKET

1919–1947

DOLLAR AMOUNTS IN BILLIONS

U. S. GROSS CAPITAL FORMATION	SOURCES OF FUNDS	INTERMEDIARY INSTITUTIONS	TYPE OF FINANCING	CORPORATE CAPITAL FORMATION
	CURRENT BUSINESS SAVING 1919-1947 34% ($262)	NONE	INTERNAL FINANCING	
PUBLIC WORKS OF ALL KINDS PLUS ALL FORMS OF DURABLE PRODUCERS GOODS PLUS HOUSING ($770)	BANK CREDIT PLUS REINVEST. OF SAVINGS ACCUM'L'D PRIOR TO 1919 40% ($310)	COMMERCIAL BANKS AND INSTITUTIONS LISTED BELOW	BANK CREDIT 15% ($115) RESIDENTIAL MORTGAGES 6% ($46) BONDS 42% ($323)	($323.7) 100% CORPORATE SAVING 81% ($262)
	CURRENT PERSONAL SAVING 1919-1947 26% ($198)	100% S. & L. 5% LIFE INS. CO. 21% M. S. BANKS 11% COM'L BANKS TIME DEP'S'TS 19% P. S. & U.S.S. BD. 10% CASH, DEMAND DEPOSITS & NON LIQUID FORMS 33%	1.2% $94 COM. 2% $15 STK.	BONDS 11.5% ($37) PREF. STK. 2.9% $94 4.6% $15

thus sought must, of course, be derived from the over-all
figures, and sources of such possible capital must be located
before attempt can be made to formulate possible measures.

Even the unsatisfactory figures we have for the cycle 1919-
1947 make a sufficiently spectacular showing as to the relative
and growing dearth of all equity capital.

From 1919 to 1947 the gross capital formation in the United States amounted to approximately $770 billion. This included public works plus all forms of durable producers' goods, plus housing. It may be taken as a rough total frame. The first question is, Where did this huge sum come from?

1. Approximately 34 per cent ($262 billion) came from current business savings. These were primarily profits and reserves made in business and retained for further investment in business, i.e., not distributed as dividends or profits.

2. Forty per cent ($310 billion) came from expansion of bank credit together with reinvestment of savings accumulated prior to 1919. (Investment prior to 1919 had been made in corporate, mortgage, and government debts; a part of these debts were paid off; and the savings thus translated into cash became available for further capital investment.) But a large part of it consisted of straight increase in bank credit in one form or another. It is fair to assume that the major increase through the bank credit route occurred during World War II as a part of war finance operations.

3. Only 26 per cent ($198 billion) represented current savings of individuals during the twenty-nine-year period. This would represent an average of about $6.8 billion a year—but averages mean little in this series since there is a violent fluctuation from years in which savings were only moderate (for instance, 1920-1921) to years when they were relatively high (1928-1929), dropping rapidly to years when such savings were substantially *nil* (1932-1933), then rising very slowly to years of moderate savings (1939), and then shooting to enormous figures (1945-1946)—the huge savings of the war years. Clearly "average" personal savings are not a good guide.

Reverting to our over-all figure of $770 billion of capital formation, the next question is where, how, and by whom was this amount "invested" in capital operations. Again the results are only approximate; they are, however, close enough to reality to furnish a working guide.

1. The 34 per cent ($262 billion) of savings originating from profits accumulated and retained by business were, of course, invested by those businesses. There was no intermediary. Because businesses do not normally act as investors in other enterprises, it is fair to assume that the enormous bulk of these savings were invested in the enterprises which accumulated them. They formed additional development or working capital—equity capital—for these businesses. There are exceptions, of course; but they are relatively rare. Venture capital was thereby provided for new and risky projects, but in practice it was limited to projects developed by or in connection with the accumulating company.

2. The 40 per cent ($310 billion) of bank credit and the repayment of accumulated savings were, of course, "invested" by commercial banks and institutions, and by bondholders. So far as commercial banks are concerned, they cannot invest in risk ventures: it is not their business. Except by inadvertence, or bad management, expansion of bank credit should not form a source of risk capital; indeed, it can do so only when an individual pledges his assets or his credit to a bank, borrows money, and risks the money in a venture. In some measure this happens from time to time; but it cannot happen in great volume. We may, therefore, dismiss the expansion of bank credit as any effective source of venture capital. Individuals holding bond or debt investments which are paid off may, of course, change from a previous investment in bonds or debt to investment in stocks or risk capital; but there is no particular reason to believe that they do do so, and considerable reason to believe that they do not. Thus, bank credit and reinvestment funds may be dismissed as a major source of equity, and especially venture, capital though minor leakages may have developed in that direction.

3. There remains the 26 per cent ($198 billion) of current individual savings. Here there is a personal "investor." What does he do?

A breakdown of the figure shows at once that the habits of the American investor are chiefly fixed in a direction quite opposite to venture capital, and he puts much of his savings into institutions which do not invest in risk ventures. Of the total personal savings ($198 billion in twenty-nine years), 5 per cent went into savings and loan associations; 21 per cent into life insurance companies; 11 per cent into mutual savings banks; 19 per cent into commercial banks and time deposits. These institutions then take over the investment function.

Ten per cent of the $198 billion gross went into United States savings bonds and postal savings; 34 per cent of the total covered the investor's needed cash on hand and demand deposits, and also his payments for various nonliquid property into which he puts his money. (A singularly large item was "investment" in down-payments for his house, his farm tractor, and perhaps his car. He needs his house and probably his car.) It is clear there is a remaining margin from which a certain amount of venture capital could be withdrawn; but it is small.

On further breakdown, it is still clearer that only the merest remnant of personal savings remains available for venture capital. This is best discovered by looking at the over-all financing during the twenty-nine-year period. For, during these years, government and business of all kinds were financed; and a record of that financing gives some light as to what actually happened. The base figure is still the $770 billion of total capital formation.

1. About 34 per cent of the total financing of the United States in this period, namely, the current business savings (retained profits and reserves, amounting to $262 billion) earned but not distributed by corporations, appears to have been used almost entirely for "internal financing"—financing the expansion of the businesses which saved the money. As noted, there is probably a small amount of leakage from this—but

it cannot have been great. Corporations and business enterprises do not usually take risk ventures in enterprises unconnected with their business.

2. About 15 per cent of the financing ($115 billion) appears to have been done by expansion of bank credit. Obviously there is little if any venture capital provided by this route.

3. Six per cent (or $46 billion) of the gross capital savings was invested in residential mortgages. The kind of investor or money which seeks to invest in a residential mortgage is certainly not seeking to invest that money in a risk venture.

4. Forty-two per cent of the gross capital formation (or $323 billion) went into bonds: Federal, state, municipal, and corporate. This money clearly was taken partly from commercial banks, savings banks, insurance companies, and institutions, partly from personal investors. Neither the commercial banks, savings banks, nor (with a very small range of exception) insurance companies take on new ventures; most of them are not allowed to do so by law. Very recently insurance companies have been empowered to take on venture capital investments in connection with housing—a highly limited and selected type of venture capital operation. For general venture capital work, however, the institutions are out of action. And, as it appears, the bulk of the individuals were looking for security, rather than risk accompanied by high profit.

5. The results are shown in the residual figure. Out of the total recorded financing in twenty-nine years, 1.2 per cent, or $9.4 billion, was invested in preferred stock; 2 per cent, or $15 billion, was invested in common stock. These two figures, taken together (3.2 per cent of the total gross capital formation), make up the "equity capital" investment.

But, as we have seen, all equity capital is not by any means "venture capital." It includes money invested in "seasoned" issues of stock—such as increased stock issues of American

Telephone & Telegraph—far more than amounts sunk in long-shot adventures like a new oil well or a new patent or a venture in foreign development.

The Twenty-Nine-Year Summary of Corporate Capital Formation

If we take, as nearly as we can deduce it, the total figure for twenty-nine years of *cash invested in corporate enterprises,* we have perhaps a reasonable picture of the available money from which both equity capital and venture capital can be drawn.

It appears that, of this total amount (approximately $323.7 billion), business savings amounted to 81 per cent of the total, or $262 billion. This is somewhat higher than an estimate by the late Randolph Paul of 70 per cent. But the evidence seems to warrant the higher figure.

In addition to this, business financed itself by issuing bonds amounting to $37 billion—this amount representing 11.5 per cent of the total corporate capital requirements. Corporations likewise sold $9.4 billion of preferred stock (2.9 per cent of total funds required) and $15 billion of common stock, representing 4.6 per cent of the total.

For practical purposes, in twenty-nine years, *individual* investment (as contrasted with *corporate* savings augmented by bank credit) accounted for only 19 per cent of the total funds required by American corporations. And of that 19 per cent, 11.5 per cent went into bonds—not at all into equity capital of any kind. From the remaining $24.4 billion, $9.4 billion (preferred stock) can be deducted. New ventures do not and cannot sell preferred stock—or only to a most limited degree.

Mention should be made of a few other sources of true venture capital, though these scarcely touch the main problem. The most important of these are:

1. The United States Government, particularly in respect

of research, experimental, and development work in connection with armaments. This is highly specialized and does not enter into the main problem.

2. An extremely limited number of foundations, as, for instance, the Mellon Institute of Technology, the Armour Institute, the Southern Research Institute, and the Midwest Research Institute in Kansas City. These foundations, on a public interest basis, endeavor to develop new products or processes and then license them for manufacture. They are tax free. But while in occasional situations this form of financing may be available, it is clearly so small a fragment of the whole that it is also not a substantial source.

3. In some cases, tax-free universities have played a little with the idea of risk capital. The idea is not likely to expand. Grants to a university have been extended to this sort of investment but guardedly and may not be allowed to continue.

Venture capital is available then only from a relatively few individuals and from corporations. In summary, from 1929 to 1947, the sources of venture capital boiled down basically to two:

1. The large amount of depreciation charges and earnings of corporations retained by them and not distributed as dividends. This was incomparably the largest single item.

2. The balance of personal savings left after the true "investment" demand had been satisfied, i.e., after the individual paid for some life insurance, put some money into the savings bank or its equivalent, or bought a United States Government or other bond. These investments of personal funds reflected a desire and no doubt a necessity for safety of capital. The small remainder was left to true ventures where the risk is high. And in respect of this, every device, financial and advertising, sound counsel, and well-regarded opinion told the individual that he ought not to take large risks unless he was a wealthy man and able to gamble.

THE DECADE: 1947–1957

By 1947, about ten years ago, analysts of capital had at length begun to be interested in capitalism's major premise. From then on we have a fairly accurate picture. The economic mapmakers in the United States Department of Commerce, probably wiser, took a manageable field of measurement: investment in corporations. Plainly the great bulk of American production (other than agriculture) was carried on by corporations. Money, the capital devoted to industrial production, flowed into and through these institutions. By looking at them, the major design of the capitalist machine could be discerned—taking capitalist life on its own terms and looking at its surface. Obviously any theoretical economist mining below the surface can discover all manner of hidden relationships, duplications, and so forth. But dealing with the current productive machine as it runs, they undertook to measure the financing of American corporations from 1947 to 1956, and tried to see where the "capital" flowing into American industrial production comes from. As noted, by now corporations accounted for so large a part of American production that the ensuing picture came close to covering most of American production of commercially current goods and services outside of agriculture.

During the decade from 1947 to 1956, American industry (this does not include financial corporations) used approximately $292 billion of capital. The important question is where this capital came from: how it was formed.

Government statisticians took two readings from different angles. The first was where the current increment of capital flowing into industry had gone—what it was used for. The second was where it came from—how it was derived. Their conclusions were interesting in and of themselves; but they become startling when questions are asked. The Department of Commerce (*Survey of Current Business,* September 1957, p. 8) concluded:

Three-fifths of all capital funds used by corporate business in the postwar period has been derived from internal sources, i.e., retained earnings and depreciation allowances. An additional one-fifth has been raised in long-term markets, with debt issues predominating, while the remainder has involved increases in short-term debt, principally accounts payable and bank debt.

In other words, three-fifths of industrial capital in the decade of its greatest expansion (indeed, the greatest expansion of production known to history) came from retained earnings and depreciation allowances (which are themselves a form of retained earnings), while another one-fifth had been borrowed, chiefly from the banks, and represented in reality an increase in bank credit equivalent to currency.

The remaining one-fifth came from the so-called "capital markets" with which we shall have to deal later.

Of interest to this study, though less important, is the destination of this capital. Here the total picture is relatively meaningless without a breakdown. Five major groups were selected by the Department of Commerce mapmakers: manufacturing and mining; railroads; other transportation; public utilities and communication; and trade (the last being the necessary apparatus of distribution).

Manufacturing and mining during this decade got an inflow of $173.3 billion of capital, and devoted $109.9 billion to plant and equipment. These enterprises increased their inventories by $29 billion, their accounts receivable by $23 billion, and their liquid and other assets by $10.9 billion. But they had got their $173 billion by retaining in the companies $58 billion of profits, by earning $52.2 billion on depreciation, by raising $24.6 billion of money through long-term debt—$24.5 billion chiefly by borrowing from the banks—and by issuing stock (risk capital) amounting to $3.2 billion. There are a couple of billions unaccounted for. Any student notes, therefore, that of $173 billion more than $110 billion (retained earnings and depreciation) was generated *inside* these corporations.

Railroads had a difficult time. They increased their corporate funds by $11.7 billion and put all of it into plant equipment. They got $4.3 billion from retained profits and $5 billion from depreciation, accounting for most of their capital inflow. They issued long-term debt for $1.4 billion as well. Internal generation of capital was about all they really had to rely on.

Other forms of transportation took in $12.5 billion and put $11.1 billion into plant and equipment. They got it by retaining $1.4 billion of profits and $6.2 billion of depreciation allowance, and borrowing at long term $2.1 billion. Another $1.1 billion they borrowed from the banks. Again, $7.6 billion (out of $11.7 billion) was internally generated.

Public utility and communications took in $55.9 billion and devoted $52 billion to plant and equipment. This is a case where internal generation of capital is not possible: rates are regulated so as to produce only a "reasonable" return. Whereas in manufacturing and trade, profit may include not merely payment of interest and dividends but also a portion set aside for capital development, public utilities cannot do this in our current financial frame. It is not surprising, therefore, to discover that their total retained profits—$1.9 billion—and their depreciation allowance—$14.5 billion—or a total of $16.4 billion as against $55.9 billion received, are low in comparison. These companies really had to go to the capital markets, i.e., they had to tap savings accumulated by (or rather as we shall later see, from) individuals. In point of fact, they issued $13.6 billion of stock, $17.7 billion of long-term debt, and borrowed $3.4 billion, chiefly from banks, a total of $34.7 billion.

Trade—distribution facilities—requires lower proportion of plant and permanent equipment, but part of its "capital" (in the financial sense) is always tied up in inventory moving through its pipelines of stores and shops toward consumers.

It really could be left out. Even there, the capital taken in was $39.3 billion, though only $14.6 billion went into plant and equipment. But of this $39 billion, it generated internally from retained profits and depreciation $26.7 billion; and borrowed $9.6 billion, chiefly from banks.

The following graph is the picture given by the Office of Business Economics of the Department of Commerce. For that purpose, the "source of funds" picture is most interesting and it justifies the quotation above: three-fifths of capital funds used by corporate business were derived from internal sources. Of the balance, roughly an additional one-fifth was borrowed at short term or from banks. The remaining one-fifth was chiefly long-term debt, plus a small amount represented by stock issues.

The total of capital accumulated by American industry during the decade 1947–1956 was, as noted, $289 billion $700 million. The table shows how it was used, and, more importantly for our study, where it came from:

CAPITAL SUPPLIED FROM INDIVIDUALS

To say that three-fifths of the capital requirements in industry and trade are provided from internal sources and another fifth from bank credit (retained profits and reserves for depreciation) is to make a sufficiently striking statement. Nevertheless, this leaves a very substantial factor ($60 billion) of "outside" capital flowing toward industry, namely, about 20 per cent of the total for the decade 1947-1956. This may be only a minority vote; but until we look at it further, it is a very respectable vote indeed. If 20 per cent of capital requirements must be raised from the outside, then the "outside" certainly has a powerful voice in affairs. Therefore it becomes important for us to see what we mean by "outside" sources. Perhaps our individual saver—who obviously does not reside

POSTWAR FINANCING OF CORPORATIONS
*Per cent Distribution of Uses and Sources of
Funds by Industry, 1947-1956*

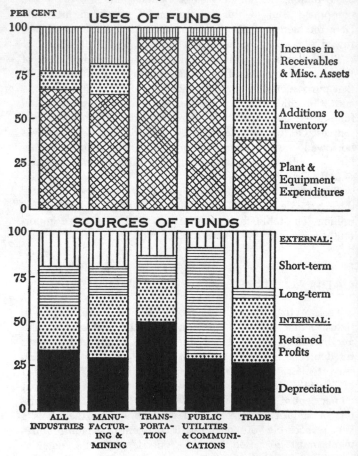

Data: OBE based on SEC & other financial data
U. S. Department of Commerce, Office of Business Economics   57-25-5

in the belly of the corporation so far as internal capital is concerned—can be discovered in this "outside" group.

He is actually there, but with a visibility so indistinct that we can hardly discover him. For the fact was that the bulk of this "outside" investment came into the market through three sources: the great insurance companies, the mutual funds, and the so-called "pension trusts."

Let us note a distinction here: presently it will be found that in this distinction lies the seed of a vital change in the realities of our economic system. Insurance is, of course, a form of saving. Roughly 80 per cent of American so-called "family units" (which, by the way, include bachelors and single women as well as families) are covered by life insurance. They do have a choice, to insure themselves or not to insure themselves. It is the only choice they do have, since having decided to insure and having decided to "save" by paying premiums to their insurance companies they then cease to have any custodial or determinative effect on what happens to their savings. The investment staffs of their respective insurance companies do that, and clearly do not consult their policyholders about it.

The beneficiary of a so-called "pension trust"—a fuller description would include not merely funds accumulated to pay old-age benefits but also benefits to be paid against hazards arising from accident or ill health—as a rule does not even have this choice. Companies, either of their own motion or in conjunction with labor unions, set up pension trusts to which contributions are obligatory. It is, in terms of economics, immaterial whether the payments are made by the company on account of its workers or are contributed to by the workers by withholding from salaries. In either case the payment into the pension trust fund is a part of the employees' compensation. It is not matter of choice with the employee. He is not asked whether he wishes to save; he is presented with employment on terms which require that he save. The amount saved by him or on his behalf is not matter over which he has control: that is settled by the terms of the arrangement, probably long before he arrives on the scene.

The assets of life insurance companies at present amount to about $100 billion and they have steadily doubled (in geometric proportion) in each decade. Pension trust funds already amount to somewhat more than $30 billion. Their increase is more spectacular, but pension trusts are young and the time will come when they level off. Since about half of the pension trusts are handled by insurance companies, the two figures overlap. Taken together and eliminating overlap, they come to approximately $15 billion.

The annual net intakes of insurance companies and of the pension trusts are, overwhelmingly, the largest single sources from which "outside" capital must be drawn. They may be called "personal savings." More accurately they might be called "savings in respect of persons." It is to these funds—insurance and pension—that a borrower goes when he wishes to make a "private placement of bonds," rather than in the "open market" as in older times. Even when a stock or bond issue is floated in the open market and purchase by individual investors is solicited, the financiers floating the issue commonly arrange to place considerable blocks of the issue with these funds. Not unnaturally as these funds increase in size there is an increasing trend toward "pure" private placement: it is handier, less expensive, more rapidly transacted, and the expensive machinery of Securities & Exchange registration and stock exchange listing, giving liquidity to the issue through a continuing current of buyers and sellers, does not have to be invoked or organized. As this trend increases, our individual saver has slipped still further into the background. He still has an element of choice—to save or not—in respect of insurance. He has not even that element if he is an employee covered by a pension trust. In his place is an administrator—it would be overstating the case to use the word "representative" —who performs the function of capital application.

Let us now combine our observations. Of the capital flowing into nonagricultural industry, 60 per cent is internally generated through profits and depreciation funds. Another 10 or 15 per cent is handled through the investment staffs of insurance companies and pension trusts. Another 20 per cent is borrowed from banks. Perhaps 5 per cent represents individuals who have saved and chosen the application of their savings.

This is the system. Further study of it may change our figures somewhat—but there is no reason to suppose that it will change the general pattern. The capital system is not in many aspects an open market system. It is an administered system. The ultimate ownership or beneficial relation to saving is so far separated from the actual use of savings that we may fairly say administration has only the vaguest relation to its supposed owners or beneficiaries.

It is allowable at this point to ask a few questions, though the answers will not be evident. For it is just possible that in talking the language of "ownership" in relation to the flow of national capital, we are talking the language of history rather than the language of reality. Is it really true, for instance, that it is the "owners" or stockholders of Standard Oil of New Jersey or General Electric, of American Telephone & Telegraph Company or General Motors, who "need" or desire to obtain additional capital? For the health of their enterprise from which they hope to extract profits in the form of dividends, unquestionably the new capital is useful and may have been necessary. But, just possibly, the real necessity lies not in the *ownership* but in the *enterprise,* or even in the community which the enterprise serves.

The pressure impelling AT&T to raise new capital (being in the public utilities industry, it cannot usually generate internally any large proportion of this capital) does not come from the desire of stockholders for larger profits. It comes primarily from the fact that more telephones are needed with corresponding increase of plant; that the community needs more communication and, by consequence, more capital invested in communication equipment. In these circumstances it is the industry, the enterprise, or possibly the function that is at stake. Theoretically, the telephone company could stop where it now is and invite some other enterprise to take over further expansion as use of its facilities increases and as population grows. Factually, this company or more accurately this congeries of related companies has undertaken to provide a service on which the American community insists. An enterprise in that position which fails to supply the demand finds itself at once in difficulties (as more than one enterprise has discovered). Indeed, we shall presently be examining whether there is not an inchoate rule compelling enterprises of that order and size to meet demands, the penalty being government intervention in varying degree of drastic quality. Possibly the question should be whether capital, represents "savings" at all, or whether it represents a variety of levy, made by the community on its production, to secure, maintain, or expand services as necessities demand.

CAPITAL APPLICATION: CREATION
AND RISK

At the outset, note was made that the method by which capital is accumulated frequently is determinative as to whether it shall be used for hazardous or nonhazardous investment. The distinction is important. Hazardous investment requires a higher degree of imagination, forethought, and often sheer faith; nonhazardous investment calls for a situation sufficiently stable so that current return and eventual repayment is reasonably foreseeable. The telephone industry is one of the very stable industries. The engineers and directors of the enterprises engaged in it can state with reasonable certainty both the physical and financial results of a given investment. By contrast a dive into the unknown field of, say, nuclear energy may have unpredictable consequences. Profit beyond dreams may result; losses may be swift and catastrophic. The risk capital willing to run hazards bears the brunt of the pioneer work: without it, new territory would not be opened either physically or scientifically.

Individuals, as a rule, do not wish to accept great hazards, and, indeed, when they do, are frequently in no position to make intelligent choice between risks worth running and risks which are not. The pitiful story of investors prior to the 1929 crash of the New York Stock Market sufficiently pointed the moral that the hazard may be great. The still more pathetic tales of individuals who bought penny mining stocks or uranium shares in the past few years sufficiently suggest how ill-equipped in the modern world any individual not a specialist is to attempt risk-capital investments. At all events, the fact is that only a tiny fragment of risk capital is ventured by individuals. The observation made that three-fifths of capital accumulation in the last decade came from internal sources of retained profit and depreciation reserves sufficiently proves that point.

For internally accumulated capital is risk capital *par excellence*. It goes into the treasuries of corporations; it is at the disposal of the managements of those corporations; it is precisely in the hands of enterprises which have already carried out risk operations and have succeeded. It may fairly be said that accumulations of this sort are primarily destined for risk-capital use. Obviously the statement has to be qualified; some of these funds may be used to pay off pre-existing debts, and some may be invested in less hazardous ways. But chiefly these funds may be used for extending operations of the enterprise accumulating them. Oil companies count on these funds for their new exploration and development work where hazard is high. Electronic companies use these funds for the development of their new processes, or for new applications of old techniques, and so forth. Indeed, one of the built-in beauties of the system lies in the fact that risk capital as it accumulates almost of necessity must be used. The compulsions of a growing industry, the ambitions of an active management, or the desires of stockholders for increased profit-making operations, all combine to require corporate staff to make use of the funds. Like the faithful servants in the New Testament parable, they must take the talents and put them to work; criticism results if they do not.

Surprisingly enough, a portion of our next item of capital formation—the pension trust block—is similarly ticketed for risk position. The pension trust is under obligation to pay a stated fraction of the wages received by the employees it covers at date of retirement. Wages have steadily increased through the years; the pension trust must do likewise. Whereas an insurance company whose obligations are commonly limited to a fixed number of dollars seeks nonhazardous investments, pension trusts are almost obliged to put a considerable part of their invested funds into the kind of investment which will grow in value. Insurance companies at a maximum may invest not more than 5 per cent of their total funds in risk operations; pension trusts on an average invest nearly 30 per cent in common stocks of one sort and another, and are headed higher—a 50 per cent ratio is frequently discussed as a norm. This is not matter of whim: it is matter of compulsion. By consequence, the pension trust by the mere nature of its being must dedicate an unstated but substantial fraction to purchases of equity shares. In practice, this means to purchases of common stocks.

The compulsion lies in the fact that the obligations of the pension trust in some measure are determined in the future—that is, in future price levels or, if you like, in future dollars. The history of prices and of the purchasing value of dollars is one of continuous (though in the United States fortunately slow) inflation taken over any long period of time. Unless American economic history reverses itself, both wages and prices will be higher a couple of decades from now than at present. Pensions based on the pay an employee will receive during the last few years of his employment will be higher. The body of assets held by the pension trust must swell up in approximately equal degree. Common stocks can do this; bonds with a fixed amount of dollars payable at maturity will not.

This might be merely matter of interesting but somewhat irrelevant mathematics, were it not for one fact in the combined economic and political structure we are considering. Common stock by custom and established habit has voting power. In last analysis this voting power can determine who shall and who shall not manage the corporation. There are few significant exceptions to this rule in the entire organizational structure of American finance.

Well, as we have seen, the pattern of the past decade (which merely intensified an apparently pre-existing pattern) was that enterprise did not finance itself in a great measure by issue of common stock. Probably study would show that the body of common stock outstanding increased relatively slowly, while assets of corporations, either because of capital internally accumulated and generated or acquired through issue of long-term debt (as in the transportation and public utilities industry), increased rapidly. The power position of common stock thus proportionately grows; but the body of common stock—actual number of shares outstanding and so forth—grows less rapidly. Pension trusts, therefore, which are growing rapidly almost of necessity must steadily increase not only their actual holdings in common stock, but their proportionate position as proprietary owners, i.e., they will hold an increasing percentage of all the common stock outstanding. Further, since their managers are prudent men, they will increase their holdings in the common stocks of the best established and most powerful corporations, that is, the corporation enterprises which carry on the basic or most essential economic functions in the United States. Even today, the ten billions or so which are devoted to common stock equities by these funds represent an appreciable potential. They do not represent a control position in a number of important industries only because pension trust managers as a rule have endeavored to avoid the power position.

Continued avoidance of that position, however, seems impractical as a permanent policy. Pension trusts grow as a matter of necessity. The investment is not matter of choice with them: they must invest as a part of the law of their being. If part of their investments must go into common stocks (as apparently they must), the time will certainly arrive when their power position cannot be avoided—unless, of course, some change in our present economic system occurs. For one thing, honest managers of funds cannot honorably refuse interest in or decline concern with management of those enterprises in which they have large investments. For another, it is too much to expect of human nature that power position will not eventually excite the interest or the ambition of men who hold it. Finally, power (though we know little about it) when locked in any group cannot easily be declined. Thus we must forecast a time when these funds now valuting to comparable size with the other great pool of private investment—insurance companies—will emerge as a major and perhaps decisive element in choosing the managers and influencing the policy of the more decisive sectors of American production.

What this new force will be remains an enigma. In point of present fact trust fund custody is held by a dozen large banks, chiefly in New York, and by ten or twelve large insurance companies. It would be easy to say that this handful of banks and insurance companies will wield the power nucleus looming over the economic horizon; certainly this is the best forward guess one can make. Probably below the surface one would find that each of these trusts was influenced in one form or another by outside parties in the form of advisory committees, investment committees, and so forth, so that factually there is greater diversity than would appear on the face of the figures. One estimate nevertheless can be hazarded with some assurance. A relatively small oligarchy of men operating in the same atmosphere, absorbing the same information, moving in the same circles and in a relatively small world knowing each other, dealing with each other, and having more in common than in difference, will hold the reins. These men by hypothesis will have no ownership relation of any sort. They will be, essentially, non-Statist civil servants—unless they abuse their power to make themselves something else.

A somewhat analogous third group is emerging: the so-called "mutual investment trusts" or "mutual funds." These are arrangements by which the individual saver may buy a share of the fund, which in turn holds a portfolio chiefly composed of common stocks. In most instances (though the arrangements vary), he may at any time withdraw his money, on being paid his pro rata share of the market value of the portfolio at date of withdrawal. The individual has choice to invest or not to invest, and to withdraw at pleasure. But while his investment is in the hands of the mutual fund, the managers of the fund perform all of the voting and other powers of the stockholder; the individual has surrendered that. These funds have proved relatively popular; the aggregate value of their portfolios is already in excess of $13 billion; they are therefore appreciable. Unlike pension trusts and insurance companies, they are not fated to grow. They may become very large, they may level off, or they may shrink. They are nevertheless beginning to be an appreciable element in potential nonindividual control of the corporations in whose securities they invest. It is too early to attempt a prediction.

THE CHAIN REACTION OF
INSTITUTIONAL POWER
AND CORPORATE CONTROL

Let us now combine certain parts of the two currents we have been studying.

We noted that the accumulation of risk capital lay primarily within the corporations who carry on the American economic functions: at all events, in the past decade three-fifths of their total addition to capital was so accumulated. This capital was constituted within corporations and is administered and expended by the managers of these corporations. Since within corporations perpetual accumulation is allowed, there is no top limit.

We have noted that the financial power to determine who shall manage a corporation and, within limits, to influence the policy of such management rests with the holders of the common stock. We have seen that the holdings of common stock are gradually—or perhaps rather rapidly—beginning to be concentrated in the professional managers of the pension trust funds and mutual funds. To a somewhat less extent, the same is true of the great insurance companies. Power over the management is power over the accumulation and handling of risk capital. We thus dimly discern the outline of a permanently concentrated group of officials, holding a paramount and virtually unchallenged power position over American industrial economy.

There is little need to argue the fact that this will be a substantial change. "Stockholders," of course, have always had this ultimate power over management. But while the stockholdings were diffused, widely separated, scattered into all manner of relatively small holdings, the stockholder in the main could not use his fractional power save in very rare instances. For practical purposes, he could vote a paper proxy for a slate commonly put up by the management or occasionally put up by some powerful contesting group. In net effect the result was that the various units of American industrial production (five hundred or at most six hundred administer approximately two-thirds of American industry) were in the main controlled by their boards of directors. The power location in stockholders was for practical purposes a fiction. The public opinion generated by stockholders probably was in the main a more effective check on management than the stockholders' votes. But directly there is a mobilization of these stockholders' voting power through accumulation of large percentages of stock, the power situation shifts. As of today, four or five pension trust or mutual fund managers, if they get together, are quite able to ignore the "management slates" for directors, get up slates of their own, and vote in their candidates. In place of the unorganized stockholders, none of whom has the energy or the money to mobilize his fellows, there are now centers of power already capable of carrying out such mobilization. Tomorrow these centers will be able, without having to ask assistance from individual stockholders, to deliver a controlling vote at will.

In terms of law, nothing apparently has changed. The corporation is still the familiar corporation. The stockholder is still the stockholder. His rights are the same as before. His vote is still a vote. The new element is that the stockholders' votes have now been more or less permanently concentrated in a relatively small number of institutions—pension trusts and (to a far less extent) insurance companies and mutual funds. This means that nuclei of power have emerged, so constructed that they cannot be readily challenged or changed.

Notable also is the fact that this is not concentration of "ownership" or, as the lawyers say, beneficial interest. It is true that the technical title to this stock carrying voting power is held by the trustees of the pension trusts, by the mutual funds, or by the directors of the insurance companies. But the ultimate product of the stock is to be divided literally among tens of millions of beneficiaries or policyholders. Property, in its ultimate sense, has been diffused. The power element has been separated from it and has been concentrated in a relatively few hands. This combination of events is more than shifting of papers, more important than mere change in stockholdings. It is the evolution of a new social-economic structure. Its effects are essentially political.

How profound this may be needs brief illustration, though illustration here must take the form of prediction of possibility rather than statement of fact. In at least one exceptional case—the Sears, Roebuck & Company pension fund—that fund steadily invested in common stock of Sears, Roebuck & Company. It now has a very large, though minority, block of that stock. Since the remaining stock is widely distributed and since the directors of Sears, Roebuck are closely allied, indeed, interlocked, with the pension trustees, the Sears, Roebuck pension trust almost unchallengeably controls Sears, Roebuck. Here is a virtually permanent location of the power inherent in that very large, very useful, and very successful concern. This case is not typical: most pension trust funds seek rather to refuse than to acquire control of the concerns whose employees they serve. More often they seek a diversified list of first-rate common stocks—the "blue chips" in the vernacular of the financial markets—and rather steadily add to their holdings year by year. At present their holdings are substantial but do not amount to control. But if the process is projected, the time is fairly foreseeable (granted continuance of the system) when the pension trusts will have the 30 or 40 per cent of stock in many of these companies needed to dominate their managements. They will also have funds available to purchase additional blocks should they desire power.

Then, the picture will be something like this. A few hundred large pension trust and mutual fund managers (perhaps far fewer than this number) would control, let us say, the hundred largest American industrial concerns. The usual consultation between large stockholders—in this case between the trustees of the pension trust funds—in each case would decide who should or should not be elected to the boards of these companies. The pension trustees are not readily susceptible to change—indeed they are in practical effect a set of big banks located chiefly in New York and a few other large financial centers. The men involved, like mutual fund administrators, are professional managers in such affairs, more or less representative of the banking and industrial world. These would have the ultimate power to determine the management and to some extent influence the policy of the bulk of the business of America unless they abuse their power. They would do so, let us assume, primarily to fulfill the obligations of their funds. But, secondarily, they could not avoid deciding by whom and in what direction these businesses (which are essentially the supply line of the United States) shall be managed.

There is ample evidence for the proposition that the institutional holders of common stock do not use, and do not wish to use, the voting power of the stock they have accumulated. They do not get together to concert action. They do not as a rule enter into proxy fights. They almost invariably vote their stock for the management slate. When they seriously dislike the managements of corporations in which they have holdings, their policy is to sell. Therefore, they say, "we cannot be considered part of the power pyramid"; and they say it in all sincerity.

Unhappily this changes neither the responsibility nor the problem. In effect, the position of the institutional managers is that they will not exercise their voting power so as seriously to affect the choice or the policies of corporate managements. The individuals for whom the institutions are fiduciaries, holders of rights in pension trusts, of shares in mutual funds, or of insurance policies, have surrendered their voting power. The institutional managers, therefore, by their policy of non-intervention, merely insulate the corporate managements from any possible action by or influence of the ultimate, beneficial "owners" of the stock. A policy of nonaction by the institutions means that the directors and managements of the corporations whose stock they hold become increasingly self-appointed and unchallengeable; while it continues, it freezes absolute power in the corporate managements. Obviously the policy could be changed; concerted action by institutional holders could freeze power in themselves. In either case, the historic field of responsibility—a group of financially interested stockholders to which each corporate management must account—is progressively being eliminated. In either case, we must deal with a phenomenon of power.

ECONOMIC POWER AND FUTURE DEVELOPMENT

Observations of this kind historically have been frightening to businessmen. To the writer this appears chiefly matter of mental habit. The same businessmen if offered an appointment as, let us say, a member of the Atomic Energy Commission or the Tennessee Valley Authority or the New York Port Authority would not become frightened. They would accept without great worry the fact that an economic responsibility was joined with a public responsibility and administration: this is the job. The alarming factor in the picture we have just painted, therefore, should not lie particularly in the fact that, suddenly, the supposed private business responsibility is seen not to be private at all. It is the fact that insensibly their position has changed.

The businessman's concern is probably justified, though the reasons commonly given for it are not. The real cause for thought arises from a deep wonder whether, in this new aspect, the power of the position is really "legitimate"—a difficult word covering a difficult subject we must later consider. After all, when a businessman accepts appointment as a member of a Port Authority, a Thruway, or the Tennessee Valley Authority, a public process has been carried out; a responsibility has been outlined; authority compatible with that responsibility has been created; the public through some accepted governmental process has approved. But in this new form of social organization, a set of more or less disparate influences have proceeded in normal course to an apex, as a result of which power has been gathered and located without process of debate, public assent, and general acceptance of the ensuing situation. This is the difference between a group of pension trustees who, let us say, in the year 1987, discover that they control General Motors, United States Steel, Standard Oil of New Jersey, and so forth, for the benefit of forty or fifty million present or prospective pensionnaires. In some natural, rather unintended, way, it would dawn on a convention of pension trustees that between the lot of them they were somehow responsible, not only for the present economic functioning of the United States through the corporations controlled, *but also for its future development because these generate and apply the risk capital whose ventures frame the economic life of the next generation as well.*

The writer ventures no opinion as to whether the process we have examined (other similar processes are working in the same direction, though the lines here chosen are perhaps the most spectacular) falls within the academic field of economics, political science, or possibly of anthropology. But because we are using power as the thread of our narrative, we had best re-create the classic phrase most descriptive: political economy. Our next essay must be analytic rather than quantitative. In this chapter we have been dealing with the re-creating of property, taking property at its face value, in the current vocabulary of our time. Now, however, we must look more closely at property, and at the individuals who affect or, perhaps more accurately, are affected by it, and seek to examine the units with which we are dealing.

11 *The Fission of Property*

THE LEGAL EVOLUTION

Present norms of capital accumulation, as we have observed, have already occasioned changes in the power relation between individuals and productive enterprise. Their continuance will make these changes more profound.

The rise of the corporate system, with attendant separation of ownership from management due to concentration of industry in the corporate form, was the first great twentieth-century change. In three decades it led to rise of autonomous corporation management. The second tendency, pooling of savings, voluntary or forced, in fiduciary institutions now is steadily separating the owner (if the stockholder can properly be called an "owner") from his residual ultimate power—that of voting for management. In effect this is gradually removing power of selecting boards of directors and managements from these managements themselves as self-perpetuating oligarchies, to a different and rising group of interests—pension trustees, mutual fund managers and (less importantly) insurance company managements.

These emerging groups are themselves self-perpetuating. Though allied to corporate managements, they are on the margin of that world, closer to the world of bankers than to the world of production and sales executives. The stockholder with a vote was first dispossessed; his vote was reduced to annual execution of a proxy directing a management-selected agent to vote for a management-designated slate. The emerging process accumulates stockholdings in fiduciary institutions and aggregates their votes. Pension trustees and insurance company managements have power (which thus far they have not exercised) to make management slates of their own and between them to elect those slates. But the return received by these institutions on these shareholdings is not theirs. It is destined for distribution among many millions of pension trust beneficiaries, mutual fund stockholders and policyholders.

Something even more significant is happening than a shift in power relations. Property (not to speak of ownership) is undergoing a profound reorganization. Its effects we can only dimly apprehend. Examination of this process must be the next subject of our study.

DIVORCE OF INDIVIDUALS FROM ECONOMIC INITIATIVE

Property is in essence relationship between an individual (or perhaps a group of individuals) and a tangible or intangible thing. (The Roman Law called it a *"Res";* the common law still does.) We have to interpret the word "thing" rather broadly. There are incorporeal as well as physical "things." Bodies of knowledge, written and unwritten, in the technical laboratories of many corporations have little physical substance, but they are so real that they can be bought and sold. Their money-worth often exceeds the worth of many items in a corporation's plant and property account, despite the accounting tradition that "conservatism" requires "patents and processes" to be carried at nominal valuation. In speaking of property, we here include incorporeal as well as corporeal items.

Both in fact and in law, the norm of property is thought to be some "thing" capable of being possessed, that is, reduced to or kept in control of an individual or individuals—the "proprietor" or in English, the "owner." In law, the essence of proprietorship was the owner's capacity to exclude everyone but himself from possession, use, or control—subject to certain overriding rights of the sovereign State. Our great-grandfathers not only owned but possessed their farms, forges, grist mills, and modest enterprises. The typical conception of private property was that of things in possession of one or more individuals. Current semantics conjures up this picture even now.

Growth of the corporate system changed that. Change was gradual and somewhat insidious. Two or three individuals "incorporated" their business; it was still small, still capable of being possessed. They were stockholders but they were also directors and managers. Legal title now inhered in the corporation; the stockholders had beneficial ownership in the corporate property and as managers had actual possession of it. So long as the business and the corporation continued small, the stockholders largely determined what the corporate title holder actually did. The fact that the unit of property had been marked for later split-up was not apparent. Enlargement of the corporation made it evident that fissures on the surface of the property represented a clear division.

The legal entity known as the corporation now emerges as an owner of the property. Any relation it had to things was necessarily carried on by individuals. The individuals became the board of directors and the officers and employees of the corporation, not its stockholders. Possession, originally the hallmark of a proprietor, now devolved on managers—at least, as long as the property was small enough so that it could be "possessed" at all.

As early as the end of the nineteenth century, many corporations had title to so many "things" that not even management could "possess" them. Top management perhaps actually "possessed" their offices and furnishings. Sub-managers, district superintendents, plant administrators, and so forth held the actual possession of the bulk of the things with which the corporation dealt—subject, it is true, to the direction of the management. But suddenly we find ourselves using different language.

Capacity to give an order in respect of property is one thing; the fact of having it in your possession is rather different. "Possession" has somehow become diluted. Under the corporate system it is no longer (assuming it still exists) the relation of man to thing; it is the relation of a man to another man, another man whose subordinate has actual control of the thing. We have begun, in a word, to encounter the vocabulary of power while thinking in terms of a property frame. The fact has diverged from the fiction.

The story that a new president of General Electric was once thrown out of the corporation's main plant at Schenectady by a night watchman who did not know him is undoubtedly apocryphal, but sufficiently illustrates the divergence. The actual possessor of the plant on that night in that case was the night watchman. The president was merely an individual who had power to give orders to the night watchman if he could make them good. He was agent of an impersonal corporation which in law was the "owner." But a corporation is at worst a legal fiction, and at strongest an impersonal entity resting on a congeries of habitual and continuing personal relationships without itself having personality.

Meanwhile we have lost our former proprietor and must go back to find him.

When our original unit of property first entered the corporate system, he held stock—pieces of paper. They conveyed to him several extremely valuable privileges. Among other things he could receive dividends as and when the corporation —that is to say, its board of directors—declared and paid them.

He could receive a share of the corporate property if it decided to go out of business, reduce its property to distributable form, and liquidate. These gave him a right to receive a fraction of current profits, and a potential share in assets in the improbable case that the corporation while still solvent determined to wind up its affairs.

His third right, valuable in certain circumstances, was the right to vote. If he held or could mobilize around him a majority of the votes inherent in shares, he could name the board of directors. He could refuse to re-elect them at the end of their stated term. This was the substitute for his former personal power to possess, to exclude others from, and to control the things which have now passed to the corporation as title holder. This capacity gave him no right whatever to a physical relationship with the things forming the corporation's assets. Ownership of a share of stock in the American Telephone & Telegraph Company gives the holder no right whatever to go off with a telephone pole.

Twentieth-century dispersion of stock and its voting rights among many thousands or hundreds of thousands of stockholders in practice commonly reduced its voting power almost to ceremonial status. But there always was possibility that a stockholder or group of stockholders or some insurgent committee could mobilize enough stockholders, aggregate enough of these vestigial rights, and emerge with power to upset management. This amounted to little more than the right to execute a very rare revolution. The widely publicized proxy fights and battles for control of management which enliven the financial pages are actually the rarest exception in corporate life. Even those, as a rule, commonly concern the small corporations. Not once in a decade is the control of a minor giant thus threatened. Managements of the major giants are, for practical purposes, impregnable.

Now this stock certificate, carrying a right to receive certain distributions and to vote, begins to split. Once it is bought by a fiduciary institution, be it pension trust, mutual fund, or insurance company, that institution becomes the "stockholder," holds legal title to the stock certificate and to its right to vote. But it has by contract dedicated the dividends or other benefits to distribution among beneficiaries under the pension contract, the fund arrangement, or the insurance policy. The one remaining power by which the recipient of corporate profits might have direct relation to corporate ownership has been divided from the benefit itself.

Actually, the division has gone deeper than that. The fiduciary recipient of dividends from a corporation no longer has relation of any kind even to the stock certificate, let alone to the corporate management; of course, far less to the real property. The beneficiary of a life insurance policy or pension trust under settled law has no interest in the stock certificates held by his pension trustees or by his life insurance company. He has only a contract (perhaps in substance a status) relationship to the pension trust or the insurance company. Even in the tenuous reasoning of the law he has ceased to have discernible relationship to the things with which the corporation works.

Divorce between the recipient of the economic profit of the corporation and the things which constitute its means of carrying on its economic function is thus complete. Management control of corporations whose stock was widely distributed accomplished a divorce *nisi prius*. Intervention of fiduciary institutions makes the divorce absolute.

DIAGRAM OF DISTRIBUTION

Let us begin by noting what happened to the things. For our unit P.P. (a possessor and a thing or body of things) represented a *Res* small enough to be possessed, i.e., to be within the personal cognizance and control of an individual.

DIVISION OF PROPERTY AND POWER UNDER THE CORPORATE SYSTEM

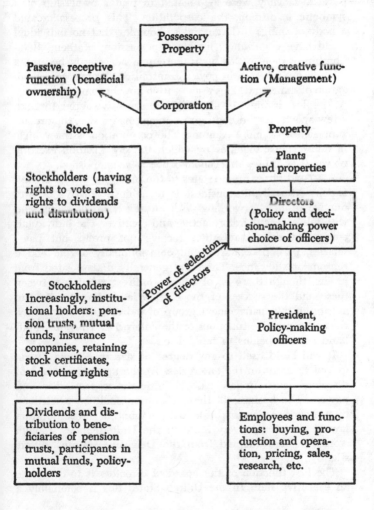

A great body of these units was detached from their former possessors. They were aggregated in titular ownership of a synthetic institution, the corporation. This process created a body of things so large and so complex that no individual could have cognizance, let alone possession, of them. Relationship of men to this body thereupon necessarily became a relationship inhering in power, transmitted through an organization of some kind. This organization now becomes important. At simplest, it might be an individual executive acting through a few agents. As the body grows in aggregate size, the organization must be more complex. The corporation is the vehicle in non-socialist societies by which the organization exerting power over things in economic use is accomplished.

A second observation relates to the functions of this organization. Primarily, its business is to achieve creative or productive results by working with an aggregate of things and with labor; it is therefore active and creative. The individuals composing the organization receive not profits but pay—salaries, perhaps bonuses, and conventionally at the end a retirement allowance. These are generally disassociated from profits, though there is, of course, indirect relation between these and the success of the enterprise. It is not unfair to ascribe to this management group of individuals, collectively, the active-creative functions of the enterprise. Thus our right-hand column begins to build itself.

It will build itself to any degree of size or complexity required to carry on the enterprise. At the apex is a board of directors which in law has the ultimate responsibility and power. "The business of the corporation shall be carried on by its board of directors" is a doctrine found in the corporation law of practically every State in the United States, though wording (here adapted from the Delaware statute) differs slightly.

The first function of the board of directors is to designate an executive staff. In the United States this is commonly a president, though he may act under some other title (for example, chairman of the board of directors). Some European cartels operate through small managing committees, composed of men trained from youth to work together with smooth efficiency and without friction; but American capitalism as a rule has not followed this form. The president almost invariably has beneath him several vice-presidents; as many, in fact, as there are divisible areas of enterprise activity. Each in turn has assistants, perhaps division chiefs; these again subdivide their work into managers, and so on down through an organization chart to foremen and workmen. Each organization is the result partly of a scheme adopted by the president and directors, partly dictated by practical necessity, and partly carried forward from the enterprise's history. In any large organization at least three, and more often four, main divisions appear close to the top. There will be a vice-president in charge of production; another in charge of sales; a third in charge of finance; and not infrequently a fourth in charge of research and development. There will commonly be many more.

Our chart looks more like that of a government organization than of a group of owners. Factually many of the problems within these pyramids on the active-creative side are essentially political in nature. One of them is "communication"— maintenance of communicated understanding so that an order or directive given from the top (or somewhere near it) shall be understood and carried out by the lower echelons. This is not a simple problem. Every experienced official has issued an order or directive at the top and has later discovered it in application at the bottom, distorted beyond belief, a strange cartoon of the original idea. Another problem, likewise political in nature, relates to keeping the organization harmonious. Within this pyramid is every tension which can arise between men. The ambitious empire-builder seeks to aggrandize his function and himself at the expense of his neighbors. Others race for opportunity to show skill or to become close to a source of higher influence or power, the object being advancement of the individual involved. *The Harvard Business Review* in 1957 published an article advising business executives in this regard; much of it is indistinguishable in atmosphere, attitude, and content from some of the chapters in Machiavelli's, *The Prince*. William H. Whyte, Jr., has described the situation in *The Organization Man*. The writer suggests that Gratian's *Manual for Courtiers* is still good reading for the junior executive. Corporation executives as individuals are not capitalists seeking profit. They are men seeking careers, in a structure offering rewards of power and position rather than profit or great wealth. Probably an exactly similiar situation prevails within any Communist commissariat.

Nor indeed are the corporation's tools so very different from the government bureaucrat's. Unlike the Communist commissar, the corporation executive does not as a rule (there have been exceptions) have power to shoot or imprison the climber, dissident, or recalcitrant. But he can downgrade him, transfer him to an unprepossessing post, or, if need be, discharge him. Dicharge may be mild enough so as not to prejudice the chances of the discharged getting another job, or it may be so handled that his business career is virtually over. The last virtually excommunicates him, not merely from his former corporate employer, but from employment in a good many other corporations as well. Naturally, if two job applicants are under consideration, one of whom is spoken well of by his previous employer while the other is given a bad write-up, the former will get the job almost as matter of course.

Political considerations come into play again when the corporation deals with organized labor. The task in negotiating any union contract for the first time is agreement with the union upon a schedule of job descriptions. The second problem is working out conditions of work and pay for each of the categories agreed on. These introduce an extraneous political force, designed to offset and modify the power of the corporation in respect of laborers up to the grade where it may be said that "labor" leaves off and "management" begins. The individuals classified as "labor" aggregate their power of not working, and place the use of that power, sometimes unwillingly, in the hands of an extraneous organization, the labor union, which exercises that power, theoretically at least, on their behalf. Power also can be both fragmented and aggregated.

We shall revert to the power factor somewhat later.

CHANGING LOCATION OF POWER

Our former owner-possessor has likewise changed position. In some ways he is harder to follow because less visible; but we can trace the main lines of his evolution through our left-hand column.

In his first stage he began by ceding his direct legal relationship to the *Res* when he turned it over to the corporation and took instead a piece of paper called a "stock certificate." But he, perhaps with his family, retained absolute stockholder control. We noted that his stock certificates represented a right to receive dividends when his board of directors declared them and a share in assets if the corporation should be liquidated (this rarely occurs in the case of any great corporation). The stock certificates also included the right to vote—which if one had more than a majority in practice meant the right to nominate and to express a choice for or against the men who are to be directors. In fact, though not in technical law, it meant power to give them orders. The voting right might or might not have any real relation to the proportion of assets he (or, in strict accuracy, his grandfather or distant predecessor in title) contributed as capital to the organization about 1918. For one thing, the handling of voting rights when a corporation is set up is itself a fine art. Sufficient illustration is the fact that under most corporation laws a Class A stock, roughly representing a contribution of $100 per share, may be allotted one vote per share, while a Class B stock, each share representing, say, a contribution of $1.00, may also have one vote. In that case (there are many of them) the Class B holder has 100 times the voting right of Class A per dollar invested. This original arrangement, set out in the certificate of incorporation, sets the stage for future development. As long as our original owner had in his own possession enough shares of stock to dominate the annual meeting, because he had a majority of votes, or so long as with three or four friends, he could accumulate a majority, he had what the financial districts call "control." Control is, quite simply, capacity to make or unmake a board of directors.

Control is a great deal, but by no means everything. Directors when he had elected them were not, and in law are not now, his "agents." They are at liberty to defy his instructions. Their judgment, not his, must govern until he replaces them. Discharge of directors appears simpler than it actually is. Stockholders who discharge directors save for weighty and adequate cause are apt to find it difficult to secure the services of other able men in their place. The banks with which the corporation deals grow nervous; banks are easily upset. As in the case of a President who wishes to throw out a Cabinet Member without damaging himself, the reasons must be cogent and the record well documented. The management responsibility, for the moment, is thrown back on controlling stockholders who may or may not have or be able to attract the requisite combination of energy, character, and talent to deal with the situation. In violent changes of management, the enterprise is apt to suffer.

Stockholder "control" in a large enterprise does not ordinarily continue for any long space of time. Normally, a generation is its span. The really great enterprises now are commonly not "stockholder controlled," though there are a few striking exceptions. The Ford Motor Company is still dominated by the Ford family, which thoughtfully retained the voting control, though it donated the bulk of Ford shares to the Ford Foundation. The DuPont de Nemours Company is still controlled by the DuPont family, through a series of devices including among others a family corporation, Christiania Securities Company. The Mellon family probably dominates Aluminum Corporation of America. In trade, the Hartford family still controls the Great Atlantic & Pacific Tea Company—a giant in its field. But these situations are exceptions among the couple of hundred authentic behemoths in American business. In any event multiplication of family offspring, time, and the ineluctable solvent power of inheritance taxes may be counted on to compel eventual dispersion.

The second stage below absolute stockholder control is called in financial markets "working control." It exists where an individual or group has less than a majority of the stock, but has sufficient affinity with or influence over the board of directors of the corporation so that existing directors will use their power to name a management slate to send out proxies to the stockholders along lines suggested by the holders of "working control." But again we have introduced an essentially political element. The focus of communication between corporation and stockholder is the corporate management, acting through its president or secretary who acts at the direction of the board of directors. A substantial percentage of stockholders with small holdings practically always can be counted on to follow the lead of the management through sheer inertia. In practice this means that they will sign and return any proxy sent them by the management. Another proportion of stockholders can be counted on to do nothing. If the votes of the group that invariably follows management are added to those of the large (though nonmajority) stockholder, the result is "working control." To maintain "working control" in this situation, the large stockholder must therefore have and hold close relationship with the management. The size of holdings needed to maintain "working control" varies inversely with the breadth of distribution, that is, the greater the number of small stockholdings of the stock of the company in question, the less stock is needed to maintain (in alliance with management) "working control."

At this stage, the "owner," if a stockholder or stockholding group can be thus described, must maintain a variety of political relationship with the management. The power is shared. The management position is quite possibly as strong as the stockholding position. Should the holder of "working control" decide to canvass his fellow stockholders for the purpose of overturning the management, the result may well be in doubt. Most of the famed "proxy contests" or struggles for control occur when a holder has or has accumulated large holdings of voting stock through less than a majority, but does not have that relationship with management which enables him through them to secure the votes of the small stockholders who habitually and blindly follow management lead. His precise purpose is to put in a management with which he will have such a relationship.

This second stage probably was the typical situation in American industry from about 1914 to 1928, though figures have never been compiled. It still exists as a major factor in a good many large corporations. Though it is continually diminishing, "working control" is a presently familiar location of industrial power.

Parenthetically, we may mark a parallel change in the social structure of the United States. At the turn of the century "absolute control"—the stockholder or group who had ceased to possess the property but could dominate any management—was probably the norm. This required concentration of stockholdings in the vaults of individuals of great wealth. It was part of the plutocratic age which prevailed through the last three decades of the nineteenth and the first decade of the twentieth century, leaving a reminiscent mark on the culture of the United States. The palace communities like Newport, Lenox, and the Massachusetts North Shore were creations of that era; it inspired literature like Edith Wharton's *The Age of Innocence*, and is well described in the early chapters of Margaret Coit's recent biography of Bernard Baruch. Henry Adams wrote of this period that in it all judgments in America were ultimately made by wealth. The picture of America as a plutocracy has survived overseas decades after the fact has passed into history. Perhaps there is a passing recrudescence of the era in Texas, due chiefly to certain accepted loopholes in income tax law, to fortunate oil discoveries, and to a mass upsurge in need for petroleum.

The decade of great expansion, the years of the First World War, and the fantastic, expansive, and catastrophic speculative years which continued until 1929 ended the existence of absolute stockholder control as a norm. It was succeeded by the "working control" stage; but by then many of the great corporations had already passed into the third phase—"management control."

"Management control" is a phrase meaning merely that no large concentrated stockholding exists which maintains a close working relationship with the management or is capable of challenging it, so that the board of directors may regularly expect a majority, composed of small and scattered holdings, to follow their lead. Thus they need not consult with anyone when making up their slates of directors, and may simply request their stockholders to sign and send in a ceremonial proxy. They select their own successors. Theoretically it is possible for someone outside management to mobilize the army of small stockholders, aggregate their votes, and displace the existing directors. But the task is huge, the expense great, and the results problematic. It has happened so rarely that the possibility may be discarded.

This is the locus of power over and the norm of control of the bulk of American industry now. Nominal power still resides in the stockholders; actual power in the board of directors. The New York Stock Exchange has calculated that there are in the United States between six and seven million holders of stock (the figure is at best an estimate). Included in this figure are a relatively small number who hold large blocks. Probably the 50,000 largest holders of stocks could still exercise a powerful force if they worked together—which they do not and probably cannot. Included in this top stratum are surviving individual holders of "working control" of which (as noted) there remain a good many; most of this second-stage group are also apparently outward bound for elimination.

Essentially these stockholders, though still politely called "owners," are passive. They have the right to receive only. The condition of their being is that they do not interfere in management. Neither in law nor, as a rule, in fact do they have that capacity. This is why under our left-hand column we designate them "passive-receptive"; any ability in them to create, or even to labor upon the *Res*, has gone out of the picture. A stockholder may, to be sure, take a job with his company. But his relation to the *Res* has become that of job-holder, not of owner. Any possibility of initiative on his part has passed. The case of the grandson of a former owner, though himself wealthy and holding a financially valuable block of stock, who must nevertheless (if he wishes a career) seek employment like everyone else, qualifying by his ability rather than by his stockholder's vote, is familiar in American business. As a creator or initiator he has been quietly displaced, just as the owner of a farm who sells it and takes a job with an adjacent factory has been displaced. His relative poverty or relative wealth has little to do with his career opportunity. These are the six or seven million "owners"—stockholders—of American industry. It had to be that way. Operating a large-unit productive system like that of present day America necessarily concentrates decision-making power while the corporate system distributes wealth.

Now appears the fourth stage. In this situation emerge the newer mechanisms, the fiduciary institutions, by which these dispersed stockholdings are once more becoming concentrated. True, the number of individuals expecting to receive benefits from the stock through the medium of these institutions is vastly increasing. But as distribution of income increases, voting power becomes increasingly concentrated.

So we discern the latest and apparently inescapable future norm in our chassé of property and power. Economic benefits by way of dividend or other distributions accruing to shares of stock are received by these impersonal institutions to be redistributed to their policyholders or to their pension beneficiaries—but wholly without direct relationship between the recipients and the stock, let alone the corporation. A pensionnaire or policyholder may conceivably have in the shadowy beyond (especially in a mutual company or cooperative) some astronomically distant and purely theoretical possibility of sharing in the assets of the insurance company or trust. But for all practical purposes he has a contract right to a stated sum of money only. His pension trust or his insurance company may have working, or even absolute, control of the Union Pacific Railroad or the United States Steel Corporation—but he has no part whatever in that. His right is to receive the face value of his insurance policy when he reaches age 65 or dies, or an annuity, or something of the sort. Or his right is to receive a pension amounting to, say, 50 per cent of his average pay for the five years preceding retirement provided he has been an employee of the corporation or possibly of the industry for a stated period of years. Put differently, his right is to receive money only, and it depends on a status position of some kind based on his having fulfilled a stated set of conditions. He would not know—and it would be immaterial if he did know—what voting power his insurance company or his pension trust held with respect to the management of Union Pacific or United States Steel. He could not influence the situation in any case. He is, if possible, more passive-receptive than ever. His relation to the "things" that make up American industry has simply ceased.

So, as noted, divorce between men and industrial things is becoming complete. A Communist revolution could not accomplish that more completely. Certainly it could not do so with the same finesse. When a Russian Communist government says to the workers that "the people" own the instruments of production but it will take care of them, it is assigning to its population a passive-receptive position closely comparable to the one we are studying. The difference lies in the fact that the criteria for reception are different, and that the political State exercises the power factor now gradually but steadily being aggregated under the American system in nonpolitical but equally impersonal fiduciary institutions.

III *The Philosophy of*
Economic Power

Economic power now becomes a crucial factor in our study. Exploration of its nature is inescapable.

The flowing tide of evolution has downgraded the traditional possessor-owners of individualist enterprise to the legal position of passive claim-holders and to the economic position of *rentiers*. Conversely, their decision-making functions have been aggregated, and have been placed in the administrations of great organizations, namely, corporations. The change has been sanctioned, perhaps encouraged, by highly permissive laws, though the antitrust laws have prevented their development to the point of monopoly. In result, the greatest part of American economic enterprise, formerly individualist, has been regrouped and consolidated into a few hundred non-Statist, collective cooperative institutions.

These clearly have economic advantage, and have produced economic benefits. All this depends on organization; but economic organization, like all organization, depends upon and generates power. To this relatively unexplored abstraction we must now turn.

Power, next to sex and love, is perhaps the oldest social phenomenon in human history. It has had comparatively little philosophical analysis. There is (so far as the writer is aware) no presently accepted theory of power, though Bertrand

Russell made some preliminary observations on the subject about twenty years ago and Professor Robert Lynd of Columbia University is presently working toward one. Karl Marx based his entire political construct on the thesis that *all* power in non-socialist society was invariably organized for the purpose of defending and maintaining the class which held and controlled property. So, he proposed abolition both of property and of the class which held it. But he did not enter deeply into the problem of power itself. Lacking a theory of power, modern political science and modern economic theory with it (in the light of present phenomena) must obviously be incomplete. How much it is needed may be judged from a comment recently made by a great European philosopher, Jacques Maritain:

The industrial regime inherited from Europe has become unrecognizable in this country [America]. It has been superseded by new economic structures which are still in the making, and in a state of fluidity, but which render both capitalism and socialism things of the past. (*Reflections on America*, Jacques Maritain, Charles Scribner's Sons, New York, 1958)

Pending development of a full-fledged theory of power, we can here merely examine specific aspects of economic power as we see it gathering in certain emerging organizations —here illustrated by the great American corporations.

SOCIAL PHENOMENA OF POWER

In passing from consideration of property and its changes to that of power, it must be noted that there is no comparable language of description. There is no unit of power measurement comparable to the inexact but revealing dollar-unit used in respect of property. The fields are incommensurate. Property can be conceived (though inexactly) as independent of specific individuals. Plants, machinery, goods in process, bank accounts, even the strategic position called "good will" can be separately examined, and all can be (albeit crudely) measured in terms of money. Power does not yield to this form of description.

Power in any form, in the writer's view, implies at least two relationships. One is that relationship which the individual or the group (possibly in the form of an institution) capable of exercising power bears to other indentifiable individuals or groups over which the power can be made effective. This is the relation commonly thought of when the word is used. A second relation is societal: how is the particular power organization related to the concurrent social-political structure?

As early as the sixteenth century, the problem of power intrigued some writers. An Emden magistrate, Johan Althaus (better known by his Latin name, "Althusius") in 1603 discussed the subject in a book: *Systematic Politics*. He divided power into two categories. The first was brute *de facto* dominion, giving capacity to give orders and have them carried out. Such power apparently rests chiefly on fear. The second was power which commanded allegiance and cooperation by inspiring loyalty to those who wielded it. Perhaps anticipating Pareto and Lasswell, Althaus thought of a nation as a commonwealth made up of a federation of communities or associations (the basic association being the family). The heads of each of these had a measure of power of this second type. These communities were themselves grouped, ascending in pyramidal form. Althaus influenced the German historian, Otto von Gierke, and through him that towering English scholar, Professor Frederic William Maitland. Our modern theory of political "pluralism," that is, of a society made up of many more or less autonomous centers of power, may in part be derived from Althaus' rationalizations.

There is no question that the elementary division proposed by the old Emden judge was accurate. A gangster with a gun or a primitive dictator with a group of mobsters can exert power; but it tends to be evanescent and limited and cannot readily be transmitted. A man holding a central position, on the other hand, who expresses or symbolizes and claims to act as representative of ideas commanding cooperation and allegiance of many, overpassing the range of his personal contact, clearly can give instructions and attain results extending over a far wider area and affecting an infinitely larger number of people. Such power can usually be transmitted from one to another individual or group who embodies or symbolizes these ideas by appropriate, perhaps ritual, action.

This second category of power is also necessarily limited in some respects. Orders given, results sought and achieved, and in some measure methods used must (at least apparently) be consonant with the core of ideas which inspire the loyalty. Effectiveness and continuity of the power itself thus rests on an ideological structure. Violation of this structure in time leads to dissolution of the allegiance, to lack of cooperation, and eventually to decay of the power.

Precisely because the scope of brute force is limited, every holder of large power, for instance a military dictator, has usually been constrained (if he has not desired) tacitly or explicitly to proclaim himself symbol and alleged servant of some set of ideas or doctrines which he expects will engage the cooperation and loyalty of those with whom he must work or deal. At the very least they should bring about the assent of those whose lives he affects.

Probably elements of both kinds of power are present in any effective organization. A gangster may induce a measure of crude ideological loyalty in his mob. The purest leader of an idealistic organization occasionally finds use for measures of compulsion. In any relationship, human or societal, there is likely to be a mixture of motives. Certainly this is true of power relationships.

Power other than that derived from immediate capacity to apply brute force can be exercised only through organization.

This means that it must be capable of partial delegation and redelegation. The greater the power, the greater the need for such delegation. Organization is essentially the mechanism by which the decisions and instructions of a central individual or group can be made causative at distant points of application. Creation and building of an organization involve aggregating and redistributing the power of individuals; this is roughly analogous to the aggregating of small units of property and redistributing its product or benefit. Each individual in the organization yields to the central source some part of his individual freedom to do as he pleases; he does this because in return he gains from it some benefit or satisfaction, economic, intellectual, or psychological, by acting as a part of the group.

Power has at least two aspects. The first is internal: the power which the central group wields over individuals within the organization; its applicability to the members of that organization and those dependent on them, such as their families. The second aspect is external: power includes capacity to affect those outside the organization, that is to say, the segments of the community not members of the organization, but whose affairs can be affected by the organization's activities.

Here we must leave the attractive field of generality, and move toward our specific problem of economic power.

POWER IN ACTION — DIRECT AND INDIRECT EFFECTS

We observed that the power of an economic organization has two areas of impact, internal and external.

Its internal power relates to the individuals within it, and is chiefly exercised in its capacity to employ or discharge and to determine conditions of employment. In respect of non-management labor this power is now becoming divided and severely restricted: part of that power has passed in most industries to organized labor. Corporations still retain it without restriction in the unorganized fields of "management" (this includes substantially everyone above the rank of foreman) and in white-collar work. Despite limitations, the power to employ and determine conditions of employment likewise includes power to promote, to give increased opportunity, to open new vistas of possibility, or perhaps to do injury to the individuals within it. These are all adjunct to the power-delegation process: they add, and are intended to be used to add, to the functional effectiveness of the organization.

An economic organization's external power is principally exercised in six ways. These are (1) its capacity to determine when, where, and how its operations will be carried on. In other words, to apply capital or resources. In a large corporation this can include capacity to build new cities or to withdraw from existing cities. (2) Its capacity to buy services, supplies or raw materials; the primary impact here is on organizations and individuals who live by selling to it, contract with it, or otherwise serve it. (3) Its capacity to determine product—a power which grows in importance as technique opens new possibilities. For this power includes not merely capacity to determine what it will produce and sell, but capacity to open (or decline to open) new areas of production as rapidly growing scientific knowledge reveals possibilities. (4) Its capacity to fix and administer its prices—a capacity vastly greater under the oligopolistic system than under the small-unit open market system dear to the classicists. As we have seen, one result is the power to form new capital with part of the price. Probably with this should be bracketed a capacity to induce consumption and sales through advertising and propaganda, though it is possible that phase of external power should be separately classified. (5) Its capacity to give or withhold dividends—that is, to determine whether and to what extent its profits shall be distributed, and to what extent these profits shall be dedicated to capital formation. (6) A new power, that of presenting a portion of its funds—commonly limited to 5 per cent of its net income before taxes—to philanthropy.

All these capacities inhered minimally in the individual owner-producer whose gradual disappearance we are witnessing. But the action of any individual in a large industry composed of small units did not as a rule produce effects sufficiently exciting or widespread to induce counteraction by any other form of power. The only substantial limitation was the effect his actions had on his own profits. Accretion of power in the great corporation radically changed that situation. It is accurate to say that as economic power has grown with the concentration of industry in large corporations, limitations on that power have emerged likewise.

One other factor must be noted: it lies on the fringe of the subject of "power." We have used the word "power" in the sense of capacity to achieve intended results. But any use of economic power (and probably of political and other forms of power as well) is remarkable for the fact that, when exercised to produce intended results, it may also cause a crop of unforeseen and unintended results. The eventual effects of these may be far greater than those actually designed. For example, the result intended by Mr. Henry Ford in the second and third decades of this century was to produce cheap automobiles, making profits for him and extending the undescribed benefits of transportation to the population of the United States. (Ford was an erratic genius animated by both motives; many businessmen would have ended with the profit motive alone.) The unintended effects included a change in the entire structure of American cities and transformation of American family life from relative immobility in its immediate neighborhood to a mobility whose implications we do not even yet comprehend.

A notable example of unintended effect may be drawn from

one use of economic power by the State. The Congress placed within the statutory power of the Federal Trade Commission under the Clayton Antitrust Law authority to outlaw certain kinds of price arrangement. The intent was to impose a legal limitation on the price-making power of corporations. In the course of a proceeding in the cement industry, the Federal Trade Commission, later supported by the Supreme Court of the United States, determined that the so-called "basing point system" of pricing was contrary to law. Translated into familiar English, this meant that a group of manufacturers could no longer adopt as a trade practice the charging to their customers (in addition to the price of goods) freight from stated centers of production, irrespective of whether the goods came from that center or from nearer points. The steel companies had regularly done this, since to the list price of their steel all of them added an item equal to freight from Pittsburgh (later, from a number of "basing points") to point of delivery, whether or not the steel came from Pittsburgh or these basing points. The Federal Trade Commission, in the cement case, by deciding that this charging of phantom freight was a violation of the Clayton Act, compelled abandonment of the practice in heavy industries generally—including steel.

The effect—it was intended—naturally gave a nearby producer of goods an advantage when he supplied nearby markets —or, if you choose, gave the consumer an advantage of he bought from a nearby producer because he would not have to pay so much freight. But the unintended effect was virtually to change the whole pattern of production in heavy industries. The basing-point system had favored and protected centralization of heavy industry at specific points. For instance, it had permitted steel made at Pittsburgh to compete in distant areas with steel made in those areas by wiping out the geographic (and freight) advantage which the nearby plant would have over the Pittsburgh plant. Elimination of this advantage favored building heavy industry plants close to markets. The result was to cause a trend toward decentralization of heavy industry and location of plant units near each major market, and a trend against their historic centralization in certain districts, notably the Pittsburgh-Great Lakes region.

The point is not that the decision was unsound; the writer personally believes it was right, both technically under the antitrust laws and as a matter of economics. The point is rather that a bit of economic power, in this case wielded by a government agency and intended to foster competition, caused the beginning of a large-scale shift in the economic and social structure of the United States. This, a secondary result, probably has had more far-reaching effects than the primary intended result.

Equally important effects may result from economic power wielded by a single private non-Statist organization. The plants of General Electric, for instance, are the chief economic support of a substantial number of American cities. Were a decision taken, say, to centralize production in a single electronics metropolis, the effect on the other cities in this economic orbit could be profound. Decision of a great northern corporation to establish a major plant in (for example) a relatively unindustrialized southern State could change the character and prospects of that whole region. Industrialization is one of the most far-reaching methods of altering a region and its civilization. Power to direct a substantial segment of that process toward one area or another is thus serious. Herein perhaps lies the greatest hazard of economic power. Its use to obtain an intended result may cause unforeseen effects, some of which may have sweeping impact.

Classical nineteenth-century thinking ignored rather than avoided the economic power problem. It considered (perhaps incorrectly as Professor Edward S. Mason maintains) economic power as ultimately and irresistibly controlled by the force of an impersonal open market. It found comfort in the belief that *all* results since they were obtained through or controlled by the open market balance were in general beneficial. In any event they were the best obtainable. But in fact these results were anything but beneficial to great masses of people. They increasingly became intolerable to great numbers. Yet revolt against these results, or attempts to modify or palliate them, necessarily had to be directed, not alone against governments (which claimed to have no control in the matter) but against a social system which refused to accept any idea or admit any possibility of control than that of open market. Thus, no way other than revolution was indicated for relief from rarely pleasant and often hideous conditions under which industrial labor was expected to work. Still less was any remedy offered from the capricious fluctuations of commodity prices which made life difficult for many of the merchants and for much of agriculture. It remained for the twentieth century to pay the shot. The situation in fact from 1917 to 1950 produced revolutions throughout most of the world in varying degrees of intensity. These were violent in the Soviet Union, Italy, Spain, Germany, and China; peaceful in France and Great Britain. The United States, after its peculiar habit, achieved its change piecemeal, partly through political action and partly by evolution of the system we are here considering.

Location of American economic power in mid-twentieth century, by contrast, became anything but impersonal. I think this a solid advantage. The pyramids of corporate power and the men or groups who manage them are perfectly well known. The men and groups who manage the financial or property-distributing organizations, such as insurance companies and pension trusts, are wholly ascertainable. The government agencies which have been given authority over any phases are steadily in the public eye. The system of production has proved adequate. The system of distribution, through wages on the one hand and through profits filtered through dividends, insurance companies, pension trusts, and so forth on the other, has been on the whole satisfactory. The policies of the institutions and the institutions themselves are capable of modification as community ideas change. Save that the community through the State will intervene to prevent monopoly, there is no apparent desire, and not much reason, to try to break up great economic organizations. When they do not perform satisfactorily, the most obvious remedy at present is not to change the system but to change the managers.

If we have lost the nineteenth-century comfort of thinking that the voice of the open economic market is regnant and is the voice of God, we have at least gained the twentieth-century comfort of believing that inadequacies and inequities can be remedied, and that we know where to go to get relief.

LIMITATION AND CONTROL
OF ECONOMIC POWER

Economic power, far-reaching though it can be, is decidedly more limited than the vast and unsolved enigma of power in general. It is never absolute. True, in combination with military, police, or political power, the resulting power complex can become virtually unlimited. (Such a combination has been used to win wars: notably World War I when its use against Germany by the Allied Powers probably was decisive. It has been used to maintain dictatorship for forty years in Russia and for a decade in China.)

Absent combination with other forms, economic power is indeed impressive but not uncontrollable. Through it, for example, the great trades unions of today have been able to raise pay and living standards of vast masses of workers, and can, perhaps, oppress them. It is conceivable that sufficiently concentrated economic power could cause the overthrow of a political governing system; but even Lenin asserted that this could not occur if the government maintained control over effective military power.

The Great Limitation: Pluralism, Including Competition

No organization wielding economic power is disassociated from other organizations likewise wielding economic power (actual or potential competitors, suppliers, large buyers, and so forth), or from other institutions in the community wielding other forms of power—for example, organized labor and the political State. No element of the current American industrial system is removed from contact with and dependence on other parts of that system. The relationship with and interdependence of each organization on other organizations is frequently direct and immediate, limiting its capacity to act. In contemporary United States, the power of any organization, however great and strong, is subject not only to the laws of its being but to the added limitation that failure or refusal by it to function means that some other organization—whether a competing organization or an agency of the State—will emerge, undertaking to produce, employ, supply, or distribute, that is, to provide a tolerable equivalent. The economic power of an American corporation, therefore, is capable of application only within certain limits. At present, the greatest continuous restraint on the use of economic power in the United States is its pluralism: the fact that no single organization has been permitted to grasp more than a limited number of functions, or even, as a rule, to achieve monopoly in any one function. In the main (though not universally) the result at present is an equipoise of strong organizations.

Classically, pluralism in this context means possibility of competition by rival organizations or industries. This, of course, assumes the existence, or possibility of ready creation, of competing units. In the case of a monopoly this assumption may not be valid. Consequently there is a consistent preoccupation of American politics and American law to destroy, or prevent emergence of, monopoly. This is based on the empiric fact that if there are several organizations in each field of industry, no one of them will be in a position to exercise undue pressure in any direction. Probably the theory originally was that a great number of units in an industry, with ensuing widespread competition, would always produce an optimum production based on an optimum price resulting from supply and demand, with optimum conditions for the employment of labor, and an optimum state of freedom for individuals to enter or leave the trade. Experience did not justify these assumptions. Highly competititve industries carried on by a multiplicity of small-scale producers frequently exhibited wide fluctuations in production and price and unbearable conditions of employment, while freedom to enter or leave the industry often meant little more than an annual grist of bankruptcies. Survival of the fittest may be good strategy for nature in dealing with animal and plant life. As a method of economic organization, it often proves intolerable to most of the human beings affected by it.

In place of the classical "market place conditions," the present American system of "oligopoly" has emerged: two to five powerful corporations dominating each of the most important industries. Competition exists between these units. But it is "imperfect" because (since all are working from about the same premises) the powerful organizations tend to behave in about the same way under any given set of conditions. Thus, they do not long produce at a loss. They do not exert to the full their economic power to exact top prices. They endeavor (with varying degrees of success) to maintain stable markets and prices. They tend toward continuous production. In other words, they tend toward planned and stabilized operations and prices. The protection in such a system is that each of the few large units can and will with gusto enter the field and the market of any other unit in the industry which handles its affairs badly. While the system of oligopoly does not hold out the old hope of an "optimum" set of market conditions reached through competition, it does erect a substantial limitation on the power of each unit in it. Of no less importance is the fact that it does set up a base permitting a degree of planning (that is, consensus on objectives, methods, and desired results) which affords a measure of stabilization.

The Need for Profits

A second limitation is the obvious need for profits. It is true that the profit motivation has an impact rather different from that assumed by the classical economists. Profits mean one thing to a possessor-owner who is immediately and directly enriched or impoverished. They mean another to corporation managers, executives, and laborers whose compensation is not immediately related to them. But it is still true that a non-Statist economic organization cannot continue to exist and enjoy power (let alone enhance its position) unless it makes profits. Therefore the operation of such organizations must be directed toward reaping profits, and they must move within the general limitations of the profit system. For one thing, as we have seen, formation of additional capital is now in large measure a function of the profit system. Increased capital for a corporation means increased power. Capital losses mean loss of power and eventual extinction for the organization.

The "Public Consensus"—The "Corporate Conscience"

This limitation is intangible, imponderable in character, but wholly real. It may be called limitation by "public consensus." This is the existence of a set of ideas, widely held by the community, and often by the organization itself and the men who direct it, that certain uses of power are "wrong," that is, contrary to the established interest and value system of the community. Indulgence of these ideas as limitation on economic power, and regard for them by the managers of great corporations, is sometimes called—and ridiculed as—the "corporate conscience." The ridicule is pragmatically unjusti-fied. The first sanction enforcing limitations imposed by the public consensus is a lively appreciation of that consensus by corporate managements. This is the reality of the "corporate conscience." Violation leads to loss of prestige, public stand-ing, and popular esteem for the men in the organization itself as loyalty to it is undermined. Deprivation of prestige is one of the very ancient methods by which a society enforces its value systems upon individuals and groups within it. And if loss of prestige does not produce results more acceptable to the community, other and more forceful means of imposing the ideas embodied in the public consensus of community commonly appear.

Political Intervention

Misuse of economic power may provoke a degree of irrita-tion or distress leading to the emergence or energizing of the action of a more powerful counterforce. Periodic interventions of the Government of the United States into specific economic fields have occurred where economic power was thought to have been abused or to have failed to serve the community.

The Granger movement leading to the establishment of the Interstate Commerce Commission in 1887 was such an incident. Continuing abuses of power by railroads at the turn of the century led President Roosevelt in 1903 to cause the Congress to give that Commission (that is, to take from the railroad corporation and give to the Government of the United States) power to fix railroad rates. Other notable instances were assumption of economic power by the Federal govern-ment through passage of the Public Utilities Holding Company Act of 1934, and of the Rural Electrification Act of 1935. In the first instance, the public utilities holding company pyra-mids had so exercised their power of economic control as to antagonize stockholders and investors in their enterprises on the one hand, and consumers of power on the other hand.

The ensuing reaction energized the political State. In the case of rural electrification, the public utility companies had refused, or at all events failed to satisfy, a widespread demand for electrification outside the urban areas. The resulting political clamor led the Government of the United States to construct an instrument, the Rural Electrification Authority, to enter the field itself (whereupon the utility companies suddenly discovered that they themselves were able to tackle the job). However powerless any individual may be to deal with economic organization on the economic plane, he does have, in the American democracy, a solid and respected power in the political field. If enough individuals consider that they are aggrieved, they can energize a political intervention. Our studies may have downgraded the individual as an economic factor. But he is still very much alive, visible, and active as a political factor.

Economic power thus is not only not absolute; it functions in the possibility that competing organizations or quite other forms of power—political (Statist) or organized labor—may intervene. In extreme cases (this was true in Italy in 1923) power might be seized through revolution. In American society, the ultimate limitation on economic power is the possibility of energizing, in any one of various ways, the political power of the government.

The result in modern American capitalism has thus been that the economic power even of its most powerful corporations can only be exercised within bounds. Though the area comprised within these may be large, they are remarkably restricted when compared with the area capable of being affected by other forms of power: for instance, the power of the State or the power of an army. The American industrial system presents a picture of concentration of non-Statist economic power beyond any recorded in modern history. But the greatest of American corporations—for example, the American Telephone & Telegraph Company—cannot hope to rival either in area or in scope the power of, say, a Napoleon Bonaparte or a Russian commissar. One or other or a combination of the limitations noted would prevent it.

Conceivably, the capacity of American Telephone & Telegraph·Company (the only real American monopoly) to intercept, collect, and use the information flowing over its wires, combined with its financial capacity, would permit vast extension of its power in all sorts of ways. Electronically this is quite within that corporation's physical capacity. Economically the operation is not impossible—a wire-tapping service could find plenty of customers. Yet the slightest suspicion that the American Telephone & Telegraph Company proposed to do that or anything like it would violate the public consensus. The immediate result would be a savage loss of prestige for the managers of the company. Continued, the practice would unquestionably induce Statist intervention and might well endanger the separate existence of the company itself. If the "corporate conscience" did not inhibit, political intervention would almost certainly ensue.

OF STATIST AND NON-STATIST
ECONOMIC POWER

It would be an absurd caricature of the American economic power structure to suggest that all economic power, and with it corresponding responsibility, is lodged in private (that is to say, non-Statist) corporations. Chiefly due to repeated political intervention, the American political State today exercises a great deal. It regulates the price of practically all forms of public transportation. It controls, through the indirect management of the banking system, both long-term and short-term interest rates. It outlaws a whole range of trade practices, such as private price-fixing agreements, arrangements not to compete in given territories, and (less successfully) abuse of financial strength permitting cut-throat price competition and price discrimination. In a newer and steadily growing range of specific situations, the State intervenes to provide or require production (as in the case of the Rural Electrification Authority) or to adjust current supply of product to current demand (as in the case of the oil and refined sugar industries). It fixes minimum wages for most of nonagricultural industry and attempts a roughly equivalent operation in farming by establishing prices for staple agricultural commodities. It assists in providing credit, which is the greatest single element in the housing industry. Were it possible to draw a map of the extent of American economic power, it would be found that a very substantial, though minority, proportion of such power was exercised by one or another instrumentality of the United States Government or, locally, by the governments of the various States.

Yet, I think on fair analysis two conclusions are justified. Most, though by no means all, governmental power is negatively exercised: it takes the form of prohibiting certain uses of economic power by non-Statist organizations. Direct insistence on, or requirement of, positive action is relatively rare. Second, it leaves to private organizations the main task of production, supply, and distribution, and certainly the main initiative in developing new economic areas, geographic or technical. It assumes that the profit motive will be adequate to cause performance of these functions. In most fields it does not object when the profits are generous. This last is possibly due to unconscious realization that the profit mechanism is also (as we have seen) the capital-gathering mechanism. In result, the driving force of the American system is non-Statist, and to non-Statist institutions like corporations primarily falls the power of initiative and action. The guiding and limiting power is that primarily used by the State, though in extreme cases the American State occasionally initiates, as it did in the case of Tennessee Valley Authority and, more recently, in the fields of activity opened by atomic fission and fusion, and advanced electronics.

It is appropriate here to clear up a major dispute which befogs the pages of much contemporary writing. Private corporations steadily assert that they do not want the government in business. They mean by this that they do not wish the area of their economic power diminished. The same corporations are nevertheless frequently the first to demand that the government get into business when they feel their power position threatened by forces they themselves are unable to control. They have invoked Statist economic power to keep out foreign competition through tariffs; to supply credit through government or government-guaranteed financing; sometimes (as in the oil industry) to keep production in line with demand, and so forth. Their objection therefore cannot be that exercise of economic power by the State is *per se* wrong. Equally it would be wrong to dismiss the objections of private corporations to government intervention as merely expression of self-interest. The reason they commonly give for wishing government "out of business" is abbreviated into the phrase that if the government enters into business, politics also enters. Analyzed, the real objection is not that the State must not exercise economic power, but that where economic power is exercised by the State there is danger that this power may be badly exercised or, worse still, combined with other forms of Statist power—for example, the power of the police system or of a military system.

This last objection certainly has merit. We noted some of the built-in limitations which place boundaries on economic power as such. These limitations frequently cease to apply when economic power is joined to some other form. The State might undertake to operate the American Telephone & Telegraph Company, or the National Broadcasting Company. Many governments in various parts of the world do own and operate communications, and both Britain and Canada own and operate broadcasting systems—operate them, in fact, far better than similar American systems. But there is always the inherent danger that the Federal government might wish to use the telephone and telegraph system as a means for detecting crime or ascertaining the political plans of individuals. There is always the possibility that the political State might undertake to use its broadcasting system for political propaganda. That is, there is danger that the purely economic function will be used for ends foreign to its economic purpose. This is a blueprint of the road to tyranny, as Stalin, Mussolini, and Hitler have forcefully demonstrated.

But, it seems, the nub of this objection is not exercise of economic power by the State, but rather danger of combining disparate power functions. This is a problem the American State has met before in another connection and which it tolerably well solved. It is the old constitutional problem of "separation of powers." Jeremy Bentham laid down, the Massachusetts Constitution states, and Federal constitutional thinking accepts, the principle that legislative, judicial, and executive functions and power shall not be combined. The Congress cannot judge. The Supreme Court is not empowered to legislate. The President can neither judge nor legislate. We have insisted on this system (with only occasional controversies about it) during our entire national life.

What we may be seeing in this controversy over "government in business" is the emergence of a fourth category in this doctrine of constitutional separation of powers. This is that economic power, Statist or private, must not be joined to or controlled by—nor may it control—any other form of power. Violation of this principle would be a nail in the coffin of individual freedom. The principle applies quite as much to the Interstate Commerce Commission or the Securities & Exchange Commission (both of which have economic power) as to the American Telephone & Telegraph Company or the Columbia

Broadcasting System. It is a principle which must be controlling within the State, as well as between the State and private organizations endowed with economic power.

For, if the political State could decree in any fashion that the American Telephone & Telegraph Company should employ only good Republicans or good Democrats, or that none but commentators approved by the United States Army should perform over National or Columbia Broadcasting Systems, democracy as we know it would rapidly cease to exist. In Great Britain the government-owned British Broadcasting Corporation enjoys a "constitutional" separation from British government control. Its officers can (and on occasion do) tell British Cabinet officers to keep their hands off their programs. Americans prefer to do this at second remove by keeping our broadcasting companies in private hands and constitutionally limiting the government from interfering with their freedom of speech.

But the doctrine must surely apply with no less force when the State is not involved at all. If the Standard Oil Company of New Jersey were ever (it has not) to indulge the inconceivable folly of decreeing that no Negro should buy its gasoline at any of its stations—adding to its economic function of supplying oil the quite different function of regulating race relations—it would violate just this same principle. Probably it would promptly be prevented from doing so by political intervention in the form of law.

The point need not be labored. The primary consideration is not that the State shall not have economic power. It is that economic power exercised either by the State or by non-Statist organizations shall not be combined with any other form of power, or used for other than economic ends. Otherwise, there is inherent danger to individuality, which our government and our economic system are designed to serve. There is also the fact that combinations of power have no visible limit; they are capable of being extended over huge areas and huge masses of men. If the State can carry on economic functions more efficiently than corporations, there is no reason why it should not fulfill them; but there are powerful reasons why, in doing so, the exercise of the function should not be mixed with or perverted by other functions of government.

"LEGITIMACY"

Concentrated economic power, whether held by private organizations and directed by their chiefs, or by the State and its chiefs, raises at once the question of "legitimacy."

Why be concerned with "legitimacy"? What difference does it make? Power comes to rest in the hands of specific groups; why not accept the fact, dealing with it merely as a fact? The answer is deeply rooted in immemorial custom and human experience. Power is a fact; but it is also a fact that the human mind apparently cannot be wholly or permanently inhibited from asking certain questions. Why should this man, or this group, hold power—instead of some other, possibly more attractive, individual or group? The human animal has always endeavored to answer his own question: power lies there because the holder is entitled to it by some test or standard. This carries a necessary corollary: the holder can be deprived of it if demonstration is made that there is no title or right in his possession of it. There is, I think, no instance in history in which any group, great or small, has not set up some theory of right to power. A feudal prince derived his right from his overlord, who in turn claimed to derive it from God. Even pirate chieftains in the days of the Spanish Main claimed right because they were stronger in battle or abler in planning operations and had thereby gained assent of their associates to their command. Revolutionary societies like that of France in 1793 or of the Soviet Union in 1918 promptly invent and set up standards of their own devising; in Communist countries today the holding of power is legitimatized on the theory that the holders support and serve the Communist revolution. In a democracy, the public consensus is the final arbiter; its will is expressed through the State or through free acquiescence. At all events, and for whatever reason, the problem historically has always existed overtly or covertly.

"Legitimacy" may be defined as the rightful possession of power. "Legitimate use" of power means its rightful use.

Legitimacy thus assumes a referent or standard extraneous to the power itself. It assumes a criterion of judgment. In a democracy, this can only be developed and applied by a community which has reached or can reach a consensus of opinion as to "rightful" and "wrongful," both as to possession and use. In a democratic society no instrument other than this "public consensus" has been devised. It is not within the scope of this essay to examine the nature of "public consensus," though the subject is passionately interesting and needs intensive thought. In the humbler field of our own exploration, that is, the legitimacy of economic power, we may take public consensus and the standards it sets up for possession and use of power as we find them in contemporary society. Public consensus itself, of course, is subject to constant examination, criticism, and evolution. Individuals, more advanced in thinking and insight, can, should, and do insist that the consensus on any subject shall change, expand, or raise its standards; this is one of the reasons why a democratic society must protect freedom of thought, speech, and criticism, and encourage study, learning, and speculation.

The concept of legitimacy is applicable to two phases of economic (indeed, of most) power relationships. The first is the legitimacy of its exercise by any given institution or individuals. The second is the legitimacy of the existence and use of the power itself.

It is usually considered tactless, sometimes even dangerous, to raise any problem of legitimacy in connection with an established system even when the system has little to fear. In justification for discussing it here, let it be observed that in every generation in America this question has come up; it is a part of the continuing revolution which has made America great. Legitimacy of inherited great wealth was widely discussed at the beginning of the twentieth century. Were the privileges and powers of great wealth legitimately held and enjoyed by men who had not earned it or worked for it? The result was adoption, first temporarily and then permanently, in 1916 of inheritance tax laws which substantially modified that particular feature of the property system. It was raised in respect of the power of commercial monopolies: the discussion led to passage of the Sherman Antitrust Law of 1890. If, therefore, a related question—concentration of power in great organizations—is here discussed, we are at least squarely within an ancient American tradition.

One approach to the problem of "legitimacy" as applied to economic power may be made through the conception of "function." Power (aside from its crude or brute form) cannot exist apart from some idea or principle justifying it and, therefore, entitling holders of it to expect allegiance and cooperation. Economic power is justified chiefly by the fact that it is needed to produce, supply, and distribute goods and services, and to set up attendant conditions of employment and service appropriate to these ends. So long as an economic organization, Statist or non-Statist, acquires and uses its power to perform this function, it holds and is using the tool for the purpose which justifies its existence. Whenever it uses the power tool beyond the area of its function, it is using the power in a realm not comprehended within its central idea. The function of a telephone company, for example, is to supply communication. Its powers are intended to be used to that end. Its operations will be entirely legitimate doing what is appropriate. But a management dedicated to the business of providing communications would violate the reason for its being and the ideas and conceptions of its whole organization if it endeavored to use its power and convert that organization into a wire-tapping service. Even if the cooperative loyalty (frequently called "morale") which holds an organization together were not disrupted, probably the community reaction would be so violent as to produce State intervention of some kind. Or, possibly, telephone communication would wither to a point where profits fell off. In any event, the economic power of the organization would soon be threatened from some quarter.

Are the functions of American corporations well enough defined so that the test can be applied? No definition is contained in their constitutive statute. Their certificates of incorporation give them permission to do practically everything not prohibited by law. (Indeed, such certificates, after setting out all the purposes and powers the draftsman can think of, commonly add a catch-all clause authorizing it to carry on any other business, hold property of every class and description without limit, make and perform contracts of every kind in each State, district, territory and/or possession of the United States and in each foreign country and colony thereof. They wind up by saying that the enumeration of any specific power shall not be held to limit or restrict in any way the powers of the company.) Obviously the "function" is not stated in the corporation papers—these merely authorize the concern or the enterprise, in corporate form, to sally forth and engage in any kind or combination of unprohibited business, for an unlimited time and without limitation of geography or possible accumulation of assets. Functional definition begins when the corporation actually tackles a project and assumes the enterpriser's obligation, economic or ethical, to its stockholders of record, to the community, or the business world, of carrying it out. This is legitimate: the American consumer accepts enterprise in corporate form as a way of getting its economic decrees fulfilled.

Thence forward, the function grows as the enterprise develops. As its importance increases, the corporation comes to be relied on by the community. The corporation sells sugar or aluminum: this is where sugar or aluminum can be obtained. When the enterprise attains significant size or supplies a substantial share of the market, it may and frequently does become increasingly essential to the community. At that stage, failure to perform its function may mean at best a measure of public inconvenience, at worst public hardship or downright distress. The corporation having won its place in the economic system must fill it. Filling its chosen place, at each stage of the proceeding, is its function. The enterprise, depending on conditions, may have concurrent capacity, and in some cases may find itself under the positive duty, of expanding its production and perhaps of entering into collateral or new enterprises enlarging or adding to its existing function.

The first test of "legitimacy," as applied to the existence and use of power, is whether the power is appropriate to the function of the organization.

The function of the American Telephone & Telegraph Company, for example, is to provide means for communication in certain ways. It has acquired, and the consensus of community opinion approves, its attainment and use of power for that purpose. Whatever it does is *prima facie* "legitimate" to the extent that it forwards or assists the work of providing and maintaining communication facilities. Clearly this includes not merely direct provision of telephone and wire services, but the myriad related activities ranging from laboratory research to publishing telephone directories or training employees.

But actual power acquired in building so strong and important a system can, obviously, be used beyond the fulfillment of the corporation's function. Power is rarely if ever exactly fitted to function; most power can be used in many ways. Power needed to provide and maintain communications manifestly includes power to intercept and record them, and to make nonfunctional use of the result—for example, provide information to income tax authorities, local police, stock exchange speculators, or blackmailers. The power is necessary to the communications function; but in thus misusing it, the enterprise overpasses its function. Its use then becomes illegitimate.

Included in the concept of function is that of making profits, partly for the purpose of distributing income in accordance with public consensus, and partly to the end that the enterprise may continue to exist, to build capital and finance expansion, and to increase the area of its serviceability. This may give it power to exact from its customers higher prices than are needed or are acceptable to the community—that is, to commit a variety of extortion and to distribute the proceeds either legally to its shareholders or illegally through exorbitant payments to an inside group. In this case, the price-collecting power is used beyond functional requirements, and the legitimacy of its use becomes questionable.

A well-understood illustration of illegitimate use of economic power has been crystallized in one line of decisions under the Federal antitrust laws. These set up the doctrine outlawing so-called "tying" contracts. The seller of a hi-fidelity record-changer may not require, as condition of sale, that the buyer will only use records manufactured by the selling company. A railroad selling land may not require, in connection with the sale, agreement by the buyer that he will ship goods only over the lines of that railroad. A producer of motion-picture films may not require that a motion-picture theatre exhibiting some of its films shall agree to exhibit all of them. This is, to be sure, technical antitrust law. But the rationale causing the antitrust laws to be thus interpreted is plain enough. Sale of wanted goods or services is legitimate functional use of economic power. Conditioning the sale of a wanted article or service on purchase of an unwanted article or service extends the use of the power beyond the function of an enterprise. That use of the power becomes illegitimate.

Clear lines of acceptable and unacceptable use of power obviously are wanting, but the main directions are fairly well understood. Most growing organizations must meet new problems, often in grey areas where distinctions are not clear-cut. Exercise of power, like the economic function itself, is continuous, frequently expanding, and almost invariably changing as circumstances change. But as a generality, there is a clear and recognizable distinction between economic power used to carry out or reasonably extend a function, and economic power used for entirely other reasons.

The other application of the concept of legitimacy relates to the right of a group or individuals within an institution to hold the power inherent in it. This merely means at present that the men vested with economic power—because they hold a position in a corporation or other economic organization —got it by a method which the community recognizes: through prescribed or accepted process or ritual. Boards of directors of large corporations are recognized as representing the stockholders because they have received the votes of holders of a sufficient number of shares to elect. The ritual of their election is ordinarily casting of a ballot for them, at a stockholders' meeting held for that purpose. It is not an impressive ritual. The president of the corporation is then chosen and invested with power by vote of the directors. This is a far cry from the ritual coronation of a king, claiming power by inheritance and the grace of God, and assuming it in an abbey or cathedral by dramatic ceremony. Yet the rationale of the stockholders' meeting and of the coronation is the same. In both cases the ceremony is intended to affirm that this man or this group legitimately holds power under accepted conceptions. It is designed to induce (as indeed it does) general acceptance that the power has been well and truly located in the specific individual or individuals involved.

Unlike medieval princes, modern holders of economic power cannot now claim God as their source—though on one famous occasion in 1903 an American businessman somewhat surprisingly did assert something very like it. Traditionally, American corporation managers claim to have mandates from the shareholders, evidenced by a stockholders' vote. Where the stockholders are real and they really do vote, there is a good deal to be said for the claim even though stockholders' votes are apt to be a pale affair. Stockholders can express their indifference by failing to vote. On rare occasions (recently calculated by Mr. Joseph A. Livingston [*The American Stockholder,* J. B. Lippincott, Philadelphia, 1958, pp. 46-47] at from 12 to 24 cases annually out of 3,000 annual corporate elections) a proxy fight gives them a chance to express a real choice. Nevertheless the body of shareholders having votes do at least assent that the power of the corporate institution shall be, or continue to be, vested in these particular men; and they do have a clear interest in the process.

But in the emerging situation, the individuals who have an interest in the results of management—holders of life insurance policies, beneficiaries of pension trusts, holders of participations in mutual funds—do not even know that they have such an interest. Voting is done by the insurance companies and investment trust or mutual fund managers who do not have such a direct interest. These now fulfill the ritual prerogatives of the stockholders.

The difficulty is not with the ritual process. Some ritual is always needed—if only to identify the men who hold the power, and to make precise the tenure and terms on which they hold it. The trouble is with the mandate. The nineteenth-century historical business mandate has been carried forward into the twentieth century. Today there is only a tenuous connection between the givers of the mandate, and the power granted and exercised. When a century ago a small group of stockholders assembled and entrusted their joint enterprise to a board of directors, they said in substance: "Manage this business. Make the best profit you reasonably can. Handle it so that the business will grow, and so that in one form or another we get or can get a share of the profits, which we hope will be good." No more was needed in the days of small-scale enterprise. In any case, the mandate was real. Economic power then was roughly concurrent with the scope of the business. It did not go much farther than that. Free competition and the open market automatically limited its exercise in many respects, and as a rule no one enterprise could dominate the life of the community.

Consider the difference between the corporation election of 1856 and, say, 1956—the classic year in which the late Robert Young challenged for control of the New York Central Railroad. Young asked for and got a mandate from the railroad's shareholders, partly by causing purchase of about 5 per cent of the outstanding New York Central shares by other corporations which he controlled, and partly by persuading a great many other shareholders that he could make the railroad more profitable—a prospect which events later upset. But it is hardly deniable that the New York Central Railroad was and is far more than a mere business proposition. Even in these days of railroad decline and of close regulation, the policies of that railroad materially affect a great stream of transportation vital to the northeast. They have much to do with the life of a great series of cities. The mandate from New York Central stockholders was historically, and in the case of the proxy fight in question was in fact, a mandate to make more money. But the function of the New York Central is no longer merely to make money for its shareholders—though, of course, it should do that also. It is to assure that transport needs of an entire area are met to the extent that a railroad is needed to meet them. Difficult and sometimes agonizing decisions have to be made. A foreign observer surveying the process and results of that New York Central election might be pardoned for thinking this a surprising way to run a railroad. Probably the case would be even more dramatic if the control of a great manufacturing corporation, say, United States Steel or Aluminum Company of America, had been at issue. Economic power of railroads has been clipped and constricted and much of it has been transferred to the Interstate Commerce Commission. Great manufacturing corporations in the main still enjoy much of their economic power without exterior control.

Analytically, we should say that the mandate vesting management powers in a board of directors was conferred to enable them to run a business. Now, though ritual and mandate are unchanged, the power actually is to carry on and deal with the life of an entire community, including within it direct customers and employees, and also the results which flow from availability of transport, the steadiness of employment, improvement or deterioration of service, with all the *sequelae*, known and unknown. In short, the power has outgrown the mandate; the ritual process of selection has only historical connection with the real function and concurrent power entrusted to the individuals. If we were building the American economic system anew, we might wonder whether the present system of stockholders' votes was the best way, or even a good way, of choosing managers or of locating power. It continues chiefly because no one has come up with a better scheme.

Lest there be misunderstanding, let it be stated that though methods of locating power and choosing its holders may have become obsolete by rational standards, they nevertheless work remarkably well. Community consensus has established minimum standards of capacity and acceptability for the holders of such power. These are generally taken into account by the people who operate the processes and rituals of selection. The board of directors of a great corporation, most of whose shares are widely distributed, in fact dictates the nomination of any new or successor directors. They know, probably better than the stockholders who theoretically make the choice, that the new directors they choose must at the very least be of a caliber fulfilling these community expectations. They have, it is true, power to violate these expectations by choosing men of lesser caliber or even men obviously unfit. But if they do the community is likely to indicate disapproval, sometimes in very unpleasant fashion. So a mandate, derived from obsolete processes of selection, will continue to be satisfactory for long periods of time if the men selected are acceptable by community standards.

Conventional stereotypes of "democratic procedure" are not particularly useful in dealing with this problem. Modern economic decisions (like many political decisions) increasingly turn on technical considerations and must be made by men expert in dealing with technical data. The decision of DuPont de Nemours Company, for instance, to enter the field of synthetic fibers and textiles or the decision of General Motors to schedule a production of, say, four million cars in a calendar year must be made by men capable of appraising the possibilities, the risks, and the benefits to the enterprise, and the probable effects on the community, on the market, and, in large matters, perhaps on the general economy. In growing measure, there is needed a blend of common sense, far-seeing wisdom, scientific, engineering, or other technical capacity, with a strong admixture of controlled imagination. There is no particular reason to believe that men with these combined qualities either would or could be personally popular among many thousands of shareholders. Such men are more often discovered by their peers. The directors of General Electric are, I should think, far more likely to choose a good slate of new directors than would be a committee of small stockholders. Indeed, on the relatively rare occasions when a "democratic" contest for shareholders' votes has taken place, through a campaign to secure proxies, one is struck with the fact that the campaigners rarely discuss the real issues, probably because they are too complex for easy understanding. Until the community on the one hand or the ritualistic stockholders on the other develop far more inclination and capacity for understanding difficult problems and reaching wise personnel decisions, economic power perhaps is best located in a sort of government of best minds, ultimately responsible to a community consensus which sets up general objectives, standards of performance, and results.

Despite the historical correctness of the ritual and the fidelity with which the selection process has been carried out, power legitimately vested in individuals may well come to be considered illegitimate by the community. If, for example, a well-known gangster were by some accident to be duly elected a director and duly chosen President of the United States Steel Corporation (a highly improbable occurrence), the courts in case of attack would under present law consider him entitled to the office. But the American community would not. It would demand and expect his prompt replacement by an individual fitted to the task. Ritual can invest a man as legitimate holder of power. The public consensus can and, in extreme cases, will withdraw its acceptance of him, and consider him illegitimate. If the selection could be traced to a dominant stockholder or group, they also would suffer. In an extreme case, the courts might (on a few occasions this has happened) hold these individuals liable for damage caused to the enterprise.

The worst that can be said of this situation is that it is indefinite and unsatisfactory. The best (it is a solid best) is that on the whole it has worked very well. It has often worked better when there was not concentrated control of an enterprise than when powerful controlling stockholders or groups have lawfully given a real mandate to directors, exercising their power of management selection. Directors of corporations whose control is held by the "public" (that is to say, by a great number of scattered shareholders) probably pay greater attention to the unwritten, uncrystallized, but very real, standards set up by the public consensus than do the holders of undisputed control. Controlling shareholders or groups are frequently concerned with their own financial situation and plans. Self-perpetuating boards of publicly held corporations are primarily concerned with their public position—that is, with the opinion of them formed first by the business community and later by the general community.

Corporate managements at present legitimately hold power when vested with it by established legalistic rituals. In the case of large corporations, these rituals have now become historical in character. They are only partly relevant to the actual functions carried on by the enterprise, and to the power with which they invest individuals. The mandate bestowed only partly corresponds to the power given and the task conferred. The real legitimacy of power-holding at base depends on its acceptance by the public consensus.

Public consensus is not static. It is in constant state of gradual development. The standards of performance it expects may alter. Certainly they have altered materially (and in the writer's opinion very much for the better) in the past forty years. These evolving standards may outlaw certain formerly accepted uses of power. In extreme cases they may require exclusion of certain kinds of men from exercising power at all. There is no institution or accepted process which states or determines this public consensus. None the less it is, at long last, the final arbiter of legitimacy—both of the use of power and of the right of any individual or group to hold it.

"PUBLIC CONSENSUS": REALITY OF ECONOMIC DEMOCRACY

To establish our theory of legitimacy as applied to economic power in the American economy, we have had recourse to the conception of "public consensus." We have considered public consensus, if not as originator, certainly as final arbiter of legitimacy. We have suggested that this consensus has set up, and more or less continuously develops, criteria by which the actions and results of economic power, and the men who possess it, are currently judged.

Introduction of the conception of "public consensus" is more than a mere dialectic necessity in erecting a theory of economic power under the American system. Public consensus, though it is indefinite, almost completely unorganized, and without traceable form, none the less is a hard-core fact. Every corporation executive knows this. Public relations departments and counsellors of most of the large economic organisms continuously grapple with it. "Public opinion" is sometimes misleadingly used as a synonym. Actually, public opinion is a shorthand phrase expressing the fact that a large body of the community has reached or may reach specific conclusions in some particular situation. These conclusions are spontaneously, perhaps emotionally, reached, usually from unstated but very real premises. The "public consensus" is the body of these general, unstated premises which has come to be accepted. It furnishes the basis for public opinion. Public opinion is the specific application of the tenets embodied in the public consensus to some situation which has come into general consciousness. It is, for example, a settled premise in the public consensus that corporation officers ought not to deal with the corporations they dominate to their private profit; in other words, they should be singlemindedly honest in fulfilling their trust. Because of this, when the management group of any corporation is discovered in dubious double dealing, public opinion immediately applies the principle.

Public consensus obviously is not a spontaneous fact in the minds of many individuals. It is the product of a body of thought and experience, sufficiently expressed in one form or another so that its principles are familiar to and have become accepted by those members of the community interested in the relevant field. In our case, the field is that of power of economic organisms and their administrators. It is therefore essentially a body of doctrine which has attained wide, if not general, acceptance. It is not omniscient; it constantly absorbs new thinking and draws new lessons from experience.

Let us take, for example, the case of the pyramid holding company—the system by which Samuel Insull and a number of other men built up huge combinations of economic function and power, dominated by top holding companies so that relatively tiny amount of stock ownership controlled corporations and subsidiaries to the fourth and fifth degrees, disposing of assets running into billions of dollars. The Van Sweringen railroad empire, parts of which still existed during the lifetime of the late Robert Young, was of similar construction. A body of thought, based largely on the work of the late Professor William Z. Ripley of Harvard, held (and still holds) these pyramids to be inherently dangerous. Their abuse in the era of the twenties proved them so dangerous that they were eventually outlawed in the public utility business by passage of the Public Utility Holding Company Act of 1935. It can fairly be said, I think, that in respect of pyramid holding companies, public consensus has not quite reached the point of accepting as doctrine that these were *inherently* bad or illegitimate; it can also fairly be said that public consensus does not accept them as safe or sound. There is a margin here upon which students, writers, financial analysts, businessmen, economists must work. In their studies and discussions, the results of such pyramids for good or evil are examined and stated. Presently doctrine solidifies; consensus is reached. A new criterion of judgment has been set up; in the next emergency it will be enforced by public opinion.

Who can apply this public consensus, translating it into public opinion in any given situation? Obviously it cannot be applied merely by the business community since that community is directly subject to it, though the views of leaders of the business community unquestionably enter forcefully into the consensus and their application of its doctrine is part of public opinion. But attempted application of public consensus by business groups to a specific case is likely to be suspect on the ground that such statement is self-interested. Of greater force are the conclusions of careful university professors, the reasoned opinions of specialists, the statements of responsible journalists, and at times the solid pronouncements of respected politicians. These are more likely to gain acceptance and influence events.

These, and men like them, are thus the real tribunal to which the American system is finally accountable. They are numerous. American universities are many and strong, and most of them are disinterested. These with the independent journalists provide a huge, informal, self-selected, but trained, panel. Their primary qualification is that their conclusions are dictated by their principles and by the use of their minds, and that their reactions are not and cannot be constrained. Taken together, this group, so long as its members are able to communicate their views, becomes the forum of accountability for the holding and the use of economic power. Collectively they are the developers of public consensus, the men first sought to guide the formation of public opinion to any given application.

Does this inchoate public consensus bear any relation to settled law? The answer must be that it does include settled principles of law applicable to economic power. But it also includes capacity to criticize that law. From time to time it may demand changes in existing law. It also carries capacity to insist that principles heretofore comprised only within the consensus must be added to statute or common law, enforceable by courts as well as by public opinion.

For, over and beyond the accepted or enacted provisions of law, the public consensus imposes standards of performance and conduct whose violation is likely to lead to serious consequences. One of these consequences is the near-certainty of political intervention by the State, usually in the form of investigation, enactment of a relevant statute, or emergence of a new rule through the common law courts. These standards some of us have christened "inchoate" law—rules of conduct whose disregard entails consequences almost as foreseeable as does violation of specific statutes such as the antitrust laws. One result is likely to be that the standards set up by consensus will suddenly be made into explicit law in case of abuse of power.

There is, for instance, a reasonable public consensus that it is discreditable for an owner controlling a majority of stock of a fiduciary corporation (say, an insurance company or a bank) to transfer that ownership to irresponsible or untrustworthy characters. In 1937, the majority holders of an investing company having large liquid assets sold their controlling stock to strangers without bothering to discover what the characters, or even the reputations, of the purchasers were. These strangers promptly looted the corporation, which wound up in insolvency. The trustee in bankruptcy of the corporation (he was, incidentally, a professor of law at New York University Law School) brought action for damages against the owners who had thus sold control. So far as the explicit common law then stood, an owner of stock had a clear right to sell his property to anyone who would buy. But so far as the public consensus went, a controlling owner who turned over the corporation to a set of crooks was guilty of an abuse of power. The problem was whether the law would now include, explicitly, the inchoate rule which businessmen and students had been discussing among themselves for a number of years. The New York courts did adopt the rule; Mr. Justice Walter adjudged the sellers liable to the corporation and its creditors for more than a million dollars. A rule of inchoate law thus became explicit.

Let us take a more dramatic hypothetical instance. The

United States depends largely on the United States Steel Corporation to supply a large portion of its steel. Great areas would fall into distress were the supply suddenly cut off. So far as explicit law goes, this corporation could vote to discontinue operations, go out of business, dissolve and liquidate. But there is a powerful tenet in the public consensus that the great corporations on which the American community relies for supply must meet the demand. Shortage of supply did occur in the steel industry from 1946 through 1949. The immediate result was an entire series of Senate and other investigations, a considerable political outcry, and a strong feeling that wrong had been done. Particular emphasis was laid on the fact that the steel companies had wholly underestimated the steel needed by the United States, and in accordance with this underestimate had encouraged dismantling of wartime-constructed steel plants. President Harry S. Truman in his inaugural message of January 20, 1949, indicated that he was prepared in case of necessity to recommend legislation putting the United States Government into the business of steel production—a powerful piece of State intervention. In result, the steel companies announced that they would rapidly increase their plant capacity, as in fact they did. Had the question turned, let us say, on a proposed discontinuance of the United States Steel Corporation operations, almost certainly the proposal would have included measures to take over the plants and have the job done by the State.

These two illustrations, widely differing in character, indicate the range of subjects with which the public consensus deals. They also make it plain that in our construct of public consensus there is nothing abstract or assumed. It is a continuously existent force, capable of becoming active and specific, because in a democratic system it can energize action by the State. Its developing principles are sufficiently enforced that they constitute requirements of conduct, positive and negative, capable of being classified as law, though the rules are inchoate until intervention by executive, legislative, or judicial action of the State makes them, or some of them, explicit.

Can the public consensus, as it relates to the field of economic power or any part of it, be stated, written down, or otherwise laid out for the guidance of American corporations and their administrators? None has attempted the task. The relevant explicit law, of course, can be laid out, and legal writers do so. The principles of public consensus, some of which are well enough defined as to be inchoate law, have never been stated. Yet men in each industry are fairly aware of them. With time, effort, and thought, they could manage a quite tolerable outline of the public consensus as it applies to them. Few would wish to do so: there rests in the breast of every holder of economic power (as in the breast of the holder of every other power) a vague hope that the rules of the game will never be applied to him, and a strong desire not to extend these rules if it can be avoided. But I think the time will come when manuals will be needed and will be produced. These will in effect be the systematized recording of experience and of attitudes, leading to the conclusion that in many areas actions or results apparently permissible under the rules of technical law are not acceptable according to the standards and principles of the public consensus.

This is the reality of economic democracy in the United States.

IV *The Economic Republic*

With this analysis, it is permissible to indicate the outlines of the American economic structure.

Its essential parts are visible. There are private centers of power and responsibility, great economic organizations on which the community relies for its supply of goods and services. There are also great numbers of Statist institutions, chiefly Federal, by which standards of performance are laid down, some abuses are prevented, and some functions are carried on.

The former property owner, as he loses his importance in carrying on economic initiative, is increasingly becoming important as a consumer and as a political factor through his opinions and through his vote. This combination has led men, for example, Dean Edward S. Mason of Harvard who is skeptical of the thesis here presented, nevertheless to conclude, as I think we do, that the problem is as much one for sociologists and political scientists as for economists (Edward S. Mason, "Apologetics of 'Managerialism,'" *The Journal of Business of the University of Chicago*, Vol. XXXI, No. 1, January, 1958, p. 11).

Ample evidence exists of changes in the relationship between property and power, under which American industrial activity is carried forward. We noted, as an inescapable conclusion of growing size of economic organizations, that the thrust of economic influence on life is increasingly administered by a relatively small group of individuals, and that these

117

individuals resemble a professional civil service far more than a group of property-owning and property-minded entrepreneurs. Implicit in this situation is the relative decline of the impersonal "economic balance" or "verdict of the market place." For the future, increasingly, reliance must be placed on a variety of economic organization, capable of holding and using power legitimately, of restraining its abuse or illegitimate use, and of assuming responsibility for meeting social, community, and individual needs. This is justification for the title head, "The Economic Republic."

Any economic republic is, by hypothesis, an incomplete republic. Economic organization, in American doctrine, exists to serve life, not to determine it. Few Americans accept the theories either of Karl Marx, or of other economic determinists, that social organization merely reflects economic interests. Far more convincing argument can be made that economic organization (above the lowest levels) reflects the result of desires whose sources are social and are infinitely deeper than economic motivation. In the United States the economic republic is substructure for the American republic and subordinate to it. It is appropriate, however, to observe that in other parts of the world quite formal structures of economic republics are actually coming into being as full-fledged political organizations. These constitute a new application of political thinking. In Europe three such "republics" have been born in the last decade: the "European Coal and Steel Community," the "European Atomic Energy Committee" (EURATOM), and now the European common market (EUROMART). These are separate political entities, "economic governments" by conception, title, and hypothesis. They directly and frankly attempt to give political form to economic function. Each has its autonomous council of ministers for policy decisions; each has a small commission or directing group; each has an annual assembly to which the commission is responsible and accountable; each has its court for the adjudication of disputes. In each case its task is to assure orderly, adequate, continuous performance of defined economic functions, provision of specified goods and services, and in each case the "subjects" are the enterprises, private or public, which carry on the actual operations.

Because in each of these three cases the functions entrusted to them overpass national boundaries, the emergence of these communities raises a new dimension in international affairs. Of this, Americans ought to take serious note. The United States is at present large enough so that American problems can for the time being be resolved within our nationalist frame. I hazard the guess that this will last less than a generation. In 1990 (probably a good deal earlier) not America but its economic republic will be forced to enter into much larger transnational groupings. Later the time will come when any purely national organization of economics will be regarded as a quaint antiquity.

America can still deal with economic organization (albeit incompletely and with growing international friction, as present Latin American relations indicate) on the basis of her own national structure. But it would be folly not to recognize that the problem of organization of economic power observable in the United States is rapidly becoming similar to those which have compelled formal organization of transitional economic republics beyond the seas.

An economic system, however organized, must respond to certain imperatives laid down by the community. Otherwise the community changes the system. One need not accept in its completeness Professor Karl Polanyi's thesis in *The Great Transformation* that the world-wide twentieth century economic revolution was entirely a revolt against the inadequacies, failures, and cruelties of the classic free market. Yet an impressive part of his thesis is capable of substantiation. An impressive part of the shift in American economy to large-scale organization and to a degree of stabilization of employment, price, and supply is due to attempts to escape the vagaries of the "free market." The long series of political interventions by the political government of the United States in the American economic system during the century following the Civil War illustrate the fundamental point. To survive, an economic system must satisfy the community well enough to assure its continued acceptance. Identifying these requirements with reasonable clarity is one of our tasks.

PRODUCTION

The first requirement of the American industrial system is that it shall assure continued growth of American product, accompanied by a distribution of its benefits to substantially all the American population.

To the experts recently assembled by the Rockefeller Brothers Fund committee, we are indebted for demonstration of this imperative—for imperative it is. The requirements are visibly greater than those which many of us have been content to accept up to the present. American national income prior to World War II grew at the rate of about 3 per cent a year *per capita;* economists felt comfortable and háppy on that basis. Americans rather prided themselves on the fact that they were increasing this rate, while the United Kingdom and Europe in the same era accomplished an increase of slightly less than 2 per cent. Writing for the Twentieth Century Fund, Dr. Fred Dewhurst in *America's Needs and Resources* forecast for all Americans a continuous growth in real income *per capita* of 30 per cent in a decade.

Subsequent to World War II we did rather better, approaching a 4 per cent rate of increase, though this slackens off in time of recession. It is clear, now, that a 3 per cent increase rate is not enough. For one thing, we have competition: the Soviet Union claims an increase rate of better than 7 per cent *per annum*, though the statistical base and consequently the result is not verifiable. Japanese scholars claim that Japan attained a national income increase of 5.7 per cent annually during the period 1938-1942, while the United States in that four-year period is credited with a smaller increase of 4.3 per cent *per annum* (in both cases, war compelled abnormal effort). Competition from other countries is, however, the least important element in the situation. The Rockefeller Brothers Fund panel undertook to estimate the claims which modern America is making and will continue to make on the American economic system for personal consumption, for education, medical care, social expenditures (such as roads, hospitals, and so forth), for urban renovation, and defense. At a 3 per cent rate of growth even present claims cannot now be adequately met. Essential social institutions will be skimped; desires will go unfulfilled. At a 4 per cent rate of growth, the situation can be handled but only by denying certain desires, and the result may well be an unsatisfactory compromise. A 5 per cent rate of annual income growth would be needed if the task of maintaining and advancing American civilization as we hope to see it is really to be met. This means that if the American population is to live approximately as it likes to live, is to educate its children as it wants to educate them, is to safeguard its health, is to keep up its forward technical march, is to maintain an adequate defense, is to expand and enrich the life of its universities and like institutions, and is to handle the burden of defense, it must produce and distribute at a greater rate than it has been doing heretofore.

The first imperative of the American economic republic, therefore, is to increase the growth rate of its gross national product. As the world is aware, other systems claim to be able to do this, though their ability to substantiate the claim over an extended period of time remains unproved.

CONTINUITY

The second requirement is continuity, best symbolized by the words "full employment." What is meant here is the system must not only produce but produce continuously, so that great numbers of individual lives are not unduly interrupted by halts and starts. Cycles of business with periodic and predictable depressions used to be regarded as inevitable—like regrettable natural catastrophes such as drought or tempest. Now, they are regarded by the American public conscience as immoral, and with reason. It used to be thought that periodic depression was the high but not intolerable price paid for a system in which individual choice of life and occupation was entirely free. Now it is pointed out that the individuals who pay the price, notably the unemployed, are by no stretch of imagination the individuals responsible for cyclical downturns. Their misfortune thus corresponds to no ethical fault of their own. Rather, it is considered that cyclical depression is due to faulty handling of resources and the faulty decisions of the power centers, Statist and non-Statist, in the American economic republic. Power is concentrated, and responsibility increasingly is fixed on the organizations resulting from this concentration and on the administrators who run them. "Full employment" (in conventional economics this means employment of about 96 per cent of the labor force, since 4 per cent of it consists of nonemployables, sick and temporary transitional employees) is regarded as a criterion of judgment. The American consensus considers that a system of organization which does not maintain substantially continuous full employment has, simply, failed. A government can make mistakes and commit errors (even crimes) and still survive. But a government which is unable to govern does not. An economic system which fails to maintain continuity—that is, which cannot keep the business cycle from disturbing lives and impoverishing people—is like a government which is unable to keep order. Continuity thus becomes an imperative.

INDIVIDUAL OPPORTUNITY TO PARTICIPATE

A third imperative is provision of actual, viable, individual opportunity to participate by work in the economic life of the country immediately available to anyone at all times.

This is new. It is a demand that economic justice shall be individual, not merely statistical. Our system has proceeded on the happy assumption that anyone could participate—that is, could go into business, enter an occupation or find a job whenever he wished, and buy goods or services with his pay. Statistically this has generally proved to be the case, certainly in the last decade. But the economic republic coming into existence no longer accepts mere statistical aggregates as adequate, any more than the political republic accepts such an aggregate as a fair test of adequacy in, say, criminal law. The system must provide actual opportunity for each individual. It is now not enough to say that ninety out of one hundred indivduals have it—any more than it would satisfy any American to say, cheerfully, that in our criminal courts only 5 or 10 per cent of defendants are unjustly convicted.

Fragments of this imperative have been gradually recognized as our economic-legal system has grown. For example, it is standard law that no transportation or public utility system may refuse service to any individual prepared to take and pay for it. This was recognition that an individual had economic right to enjoy the service if he could pay the price. In fact, though not yet recognized in law, this rule probably is valid in respect of nonpublic utility corporations: I should doubt whether any great company could arbitrarily refuse (without adequate cause) to sell to any individual steel or aluminum, electrical appliances or automobiles. In the field of employment, many States already make it an offense to deny employment to an individual by reason of race or religion.

Yet it is still possible for the system, as we know it, to do cruel and hideous things. Not long ago a Puerto Rican, member of a cafeteria workers' union, lost his job because his employer went out of business. He applied for and in rapid succession got two other jobs; but in each case his employment was prevented because two other unions had "jurisdiction" over the respective employers. He was not permitted to transfer freely from his union to the others (in any event it would have cost a large initiation fee). He ended on the street, with the added gratuitous cruelty that he (because he had worked two days at one of these jobs) was for the time ineligible for relief. These individual hardships are as great and as unpardonable as cases where the individual has been imprisoned for a crime which he did not commit. It would be possible, for instance, to take care of our Puerto Rican laborer by requiring (as Mr. Justice Brandeis proposed in his younger days) that every union shall be "open." Probably this will have to be supplemented by a measure advocated by the late Fiorello H. LaGuardia: a steady and continuous employment at which anyone who wishes to work at the standard minimum wage can always be employed at any time and for any length of time on simple application.

ECONOMIC PLANNING

The obvious institutional requirement to meet these three major demands is adequate organization of existing instruments of national economic planning. New organization here need not be great. The immediate need is rather to collect the large number of existing governmental agencies which happily go their independent courses all over Washington, bringing them into solid working relationship with each other and with their junior affiliates in the forty-eight States to attain defined objectives.

Planning has been fiercely controversial, as anyone who lived with and through the attempts made by President Franklin

Roosevelt along those lines will remember. Part at least of the fierce opposition arose (and still arises) from failure to understand what planning is and the extent to which American economy is already planned and charted. Opponents were fighting a bogey of Statist administration, rather than dealing with the reality of concerting powers already existing, and using measures already well understood in meeting situations for which everyone had demanded remedy.

Is objection to economic planning real or fanciful?

A congeries of powerful planning organizations already functions as part of the Government of the United States, each of them covering a sector of American economy, too often without reference to other sectors or other planning agencies. They are the results of repeated political intervention, save where they resulted from military initiative. The Granger movement brought the Interstate Commerce Commission into existence in 1887, a system obsolescent now but unquestionably of service during several decades. A second intervention, championed by President Theodore Roosevelt, brought amplification of that system through the Hepburn Act of 1903. Failure of the commercial bank system to function well in the panics of 1903 and 1907 brought about studies (headed by Republican Senator Nelson Aldrich) which led (at the insistence of a Democrat, President Woodrow Wilson) to passage of the Federal Reserve Act of 1914 and organization of the Federal Reserve Board. This has evolved through the years; at present it is a planning and control system for handling and control of currency and bank credit (with repercussions on most other varieties of credit). It is also a thoroughly accepted mechanism by which attempt is made to control disturbances in the entire economic system, using currency-credit tools for that purpose.

In 1933, the catastrophe which Winston Churchill christened "the economic blizzard" led to a wholesale political intervention in the United States engendering a whole group of measures. Notable among them was the planning mechanism for the oil industry, begun under the National Industrial Recovery Act and continued by Federal statute and interstate treaty when the N.R.A. mechanism was held unconstitutional by the Supreme Court. The Federal Power Commission was given authority to do a large amount of planning in connection with hydroelectric power through the Federal Power Commission Act of 1934. The radio broadcasting industry, which now includes television, fell under planning control through the Federal Communications Acts of 1928 and 1934, respectively; these enlarged a mechanism administratively brought into existence by President (then Secretary of Commerce) Herbert Hoover in 1928 which had fared badly in the courts. Aviation became a planned industry through a combination of mail subsidies and regulation through the Civil Aeronautics Act of 1938.

The list could be extended indefinitely, but specific note must be taken of new formations which have emerged as a result of the sunburst of technical development. The Atomic Energy Act is a specific mandate for planned development of nuclear energy. More flexible, though no less important, are the arrangements by which the Department of Defense parcels out tasks in scientific research and technical development of the discoveries made. The pattern of applied development of abstract science almost inevitably follows at least for a time the pattern of guided research and "development orders." Surveying the entire field of American industry, it becomes apparent that many of its sectors, and not the least important, are already guided, regulated, or controlled through one means or another. In each case the solution was *ad hoc*—a job done to meet a more or less specific emergency, covering a limited field. The principle of planning cannot be said to be repugnant to American political practice.

In the non-Statist area, the history of American industry

makes it quite clear that each industry will do all the planning possible, within the limitations of the antitrust laws. A monopoly, of course, has almost complete planning power; the precise reason why monopoly is outlawed by antitrust law is because, in such case, it is assumed that the planning will naturally be in the sole interest of the monopolist. Agreements between companies "in restraint of trade" are nothing else but a method by which each participant plans with others its production or its price or its territory. Again, the complaint is that private planning leaves the interest of smaller enterprises, as well as of the public, out of the picture. The conclusion seems fairly clear: the American private enterprise system is not opposed to planning either. Planning is bitterly opposed, not without reason, if it is irresponsible, such as planning in defense of special interests. It is accepted when recognized as needed to meet clear social demands. And, as we have seen, certain social demands are emerging as imperatives in the American economic scene.

The politician in these matters is commonly ahead of the scholar. He knows that violation of an imperative means a political upset of which he is likely to be victim. He therefore must drive ahead, ignoring warnings of business economists, fears of financial men, and the grave counsel of savants who point out difficulties and ask three years for research before giving an opinion. Nevertheless he must draw his plans from somewhere. He commonly seeks the assistance of men who have seriously thought about the problem, and have the daring to push ahead despite the fact that the results are by no means certain. Just such a new political push is, I think, in the making in the United States now. Some advance toward the economic republic, that is, toward organization which will meet the three presently recognized imperatives, will be devised. Our real choice now is not whether they will be met, but how they will be met.

INSTRUMENTS OF GOVERNMENT
PLANNING

To blueprint a national planning agency would be obviously impossible here but the nucleus of it is clear.

An inventory of the agencies in Washington which compile economic data would itself be long. It would disclose that the inflow of economic information is probably greater, more continuous, more detailed, and on the whole more accurate than anyone realizes. For example, if the data continuously maintained by the Federal Reserve Board, and by the Office of Business Economics of the Department of Commerce, and by the Department of the Treasury were collated, and if to these were added the data regularly accumulated through the Federal Housing Administration (in respect of housing), the Maritime Commission (in connection with shipping), the Bureau of Mines (in connection with oil), the Department of Agriculture (in connection with farm products) and of other specialized agencies, and if the whole were regularly reviewed and interpreted through, let us say, the President's Economic Advisory Committee, information needed for source planning would be readily present. Taken together, there is enough economic information regularly flowing into Washington to give an excellent picture both *en masse* and in local detail.

Second, inventory of the control agencies in Washington would develop the fact that a great part of American industry already falls within the direct or indirect limits of some form of present control. These agencies grew up historically; they are disparate. The policy of the Interstate Commerce Commission, which deals with railroads and trucks, does not have to take much account of the condition of air transport. The Civil Aeronautics Board, regulating air travel and transport, does not need to take too much account of the policies of the Maritime Commission, which in turn regulates, as it subsidizes, the American Merchant Marine. Nor do any of these necessarily have to take into account the policies of the Federal Housing Administration. My second plea is, therefore, that some method be found of bringing together the various control agencies to which the country is accustomed so that their policies may work together instead of separately.

It will rapidly be found that agencies controlling industry take several forms. The following are samples. Yet they illustrate sufficiently the fact that if used together to realize the imperatives mentioned and others as they appear, much more can be done to stimulate growth and maintain continuity. Probably these controls, fully examined, would make a schedule something like this.

1. The control of currency and credit chiefly exercised by the Federal Reserve Board.

2. The control of long-term interest rates, chiefly carried out through the Treasury through its debt management policy, but interacting materially with the so-called open market operations which the Federal Reserve Board can conduct through purchase and sale of government bonds.

3. The extension of credit, directly or through government guarantee, for specific industries through specific and more or less isolated agencies. These include, by way of illustration, the Farm loan banks and the agricultural system; the Federal Housing Administration which may make credit available for construction; the Maritime Commission which may make credit available for shipping; and various branches of the Department of Defense which through handling government orders virtually makes credit available to the defense industries. There are a dozen other agencies which do the same thing. Notable for its absence is any agency which makes credit available in large amounts for social expenditures.

4. Agencies which tend to equate production or supply with demand. The Bureau of Mines, taken together with the Interstate Oil Compact which in turn coordinates action by the

various States, endeavors to keep the supply of oil above ground in reasonable degree of steady relationship of current demand. The Department of Agriculture does the same thing with respect to imports of raw sugar. Crude as it is, the stockpiling authority chiefly held by the Department of Defense can be, and at times has been, used to absorb surpluses or shortages of a number of nonferrous metals, keeping the floating supply in reasonable range of current demand.

5. The regulatory agencies, which include again the Interstate Commerce Commission governing rail and truck transport, the Civil Aeronautics Board regulating air travel rates, the Federal Power Commission now regulating natural gas as well as electric power operations—to name a few.

6. The direct production agencies of the United States: the Tennessee Valley, Columbia River, Hoover Dam, and other similar projects. Probably the Atomic Energy Commission which also directly intervenes in production falls in this class. In other fields, the direct production agencies conducted by the Department of Defense.

This is merely a suggestion of how the task could be gone at. It would be found, I think, that if all the powers of the various agencies were handled coordinately for the purpose of providing the results in which America seeks its total economy, the actual powers already conceded to the State would not need much supplementation. Clearly in each field some additions should be considered. It has never been clear why the Federal Reserve Board should not be able, within limits, to direct credit as well as to determine its total volume; why, for example, when consumers' credit and installment buying reach dangerous levels, their authority should not be used to steer credit elsewhere, as it already steers credit away from speculative use in the stock market.

For that matter, there is some question why it is right and just to assure that the supply of oil shall be kept within reasonable distance of the consumption of oil, while the volume of automobile manufacture is supposed to be merely matter of private concern. The National City Bank some time ago estimated the solid market for cars at about six million per year. The automobile industry disagreed, and considered itself justified when in the ensuing year it sold eight million. For 1958, however, estimates were that the industry will currently sell four and a half million or perhaps less. The result has been discontinuity, with one-sixth of Detroit out of a job. It is not even necessary in cases like that of the automobile industry either to regulate price or limit production. If an economic staff were quite clear that overemphasis on automobile selling in 1956-1957 would mean discontinuity and unemployment in 1958-1959, it should be made possible for the Federal Reserve Board to arrange that credit for installment buying of new cars will be so handled as to prevent a bulge in buying one year and an extreme dip in the next. The rule in such cases could well be that any individual is free to buy anything he wishes so long as he has the money to pay for it, and any manufacturer free to manufacture whatever he thinks he can sell; but that neither buyer nor seller has a right to the facilities of Federal credit, directly or indirectly, beyond a point which appears unsafe.

INSTRUMENTS OF PRIVATE PLANNING

Concomitant with rationalizing government action, it would seem that the private centers of responsibility or of economic power might likewise be expected to convene from time to time to consider, not merely their private interests, but also their responsibilities as part of the total economy. There are endless organizations in each industry and inter-industry which could be elevated into responsible adjuncts of American policy. The Iron and Steel Institute and like institutions in other great manufacturing industries are not Statist, but they are no less a part of the economic republic. They know the impact of events on their own industry and on its functions better than any other groups. They can calculate the probable demand for their product for some years ahead, and estimate more or less reasonably the amount of capital they will need to collect and apply to satisfy the probable demands of one, three, seven, or ten years from today.

It ought to be made possible for these groups to synchronize or harmonize their own capital expenditures. This might require relief from some of the rigidities of the antitrust laws. It is reasonable to suppose that, with the assistance of an American economic planning staff, capital expenditures of all industries could be arranged so that they would not be bunched to emergency speed in some years and dangerously slacked off in others. One major cause of discontinuity and unemployment is the fact that capital is unevenly applied and expanded. Common sense would suggest that capital should be so handled as to make possible increased capital expenditures for known future needs when recession begins, and to level off capital expenditures when capacity has been created which threatens to outrun demand.

Finally, use of existing powers (some may need to be added) should make possible the steering of capital application away from commercial and into social expenditures where this becomes necessary. An obvious time to provide needed community services is when private employment slackens.

You will notice a studied endeavor to escape the classic bureaucratic form of "regulation." Aside from its infernal complexity, the modern bureaucracy is frequently irresponsible in timing; it thinks of itself not as a manager but as a court. What we really want is to have an economic planning staff which will estimate resources and needs and which will—through the operation of credit, persuasion, and common sense —make it logical for the administrators of private economic power to meet these needs. Actually the first over-all estimate of America's needs and resources in modern history was made by the Twentieth Century Fund, a private foundation, and published only in 1947. The first current estimate of America's capital requirements (it was for the period 1946-1960) was made by the same foundation and only published in 1950.

I venture the thesis that acute cyclical depressions are presently avoidable and that the American economic republic now has power to avoid them. Failure to avoid them hereafter will be due, not to lack of ability, but to unwillingness to face the issue. With government staff work and planning, and with sound working relationship between the State and the present organizations of non-Statist concentrated power, the task can be done if the United States really wishes to do it.

THE RIGHT TO WORK

The third requirement is that the economic system shall give direct available opportunity—which is the real meaning of social justice—to all individuals. Averages and statistical aggregates are no longer enough.

This is an extension of the struggle of twenty-five years ago which resulted, among other things, in the current system of social security. Then it was determined (not without opposition) that human needs must be met and that it was unjust to inflict on groups temporarily displaced through no fault of their own the burden of changes, economic or technical, or to require them to pay the price of mistakes in management. That decision was taken as a result of political conflict. A public consensus was established, and there is no chance of its reversal.

At present there is rising demand that the system go farther. Unemployment relief is all very well as a temporary expedient. But it is not a substitute for creative economic life. The British discovered that in the years following World War I when great numbers of their population lived on an indefinite dole.

This means that a combination of private, local, regional, and national operations shall be so carried on that anyone who wishes to work at the settled minimum wage rates shall receive such work at once on simple application, and that financial arrangements shall be made presumably through the Federal government to meet the cost. The task is not without difficulty; but it is far less difficult than many other tasks American managerial ability has satisfactorily solved. Some of the social expenditures which are needed can be handled in this fashion. There is no community, however small, in which an afternoon's stroll will not suggest an endless amount of work to be done. The bulk of such work would be neither capricious nor unsystematic. Perhaps we have reached a point where an old dream of the late Fiorello H. LaGuardia—work always available on simple application—can be realized.

One of the solid achievements of the Soviet State has been in this field. There, except as a result of political disgrace, theoretically at least, no individual within the Communist system is allowed to be out of a job. Here, no individual needs to be out of a job.

THE FINAL AUTHORITY

We began by observing that the individual no longer wielded significant power through productive property. He has ceased to be a true capitalist. Now, in our economic republic, we find him again. Accurately apprehended and depending on his choice of life values and of the life he chooses to lead, he can be and indeed is the final authority.

It is not necessary here to repeat a theoretical analysis made by the writer some years ago in *The Natural Selection of Political Forces*. The conclusion there was that every organization (this is true of our own economic republic) essentially gives form to a core of conceptions and ideas—the same conceptions and ideas which appear in this analysis as "public consensus." In a democracy, this core of ideas, conceptions, and desires is a consensus of choices made by individuals who seek illumination, guidance, perhaps leadership from men they trust, as to the life values they hope to realize. But leadership toward and development of a consensus of opinion on life values are not the product of the centers of power and responsibility directing the economic machinery. They come out of the universities and institutions of learning, the daily and periodical press, the authors who write more formally in books. Occasionally, the men who lead may take office in public life, or even directorships in corporations; but their dedication is to humanity and truth. They are our spiritual élite. Over the years an Albert Schweitzer or a William James, a Eugene O'Neill or a John Dewey has more causative power than all the Lords Temporal of economic institutions.

In little or in great, every individual has within himself the power to be a member of this élite. If he no longer dominates conditions under which he makes his living, he can always dominate the principle on which he will make his life. A truckdriver has (approximately) the income of an assistant professor at Princeton. He can, if he chooses, make a life comparable to that found on the borders of any campus. The aggregate of these personal choices determines the currents of what economists call "consumption." In final account, they govern the product and operations of the industrial apparatus, which must, ultimately, meet the level of individual choice.

It is easy to say that in so large a country there is no individual choice—merely the choice made by a mass; and that masses are not to be trusted. This is an old argument, carried on when democracy was young and frightening. You will find it considered in Book II of Montesquieu's *Spirit of Laws,* and in Jefferson's writings when the American republic was young.

Closer students find less to fear than to hope. For example, one of the more interesting minor statistics is the fact that in recent years more Americans paid for tickets to classical concerts than for tickets to baseball games. There is a persistent tendency to underestimate both the capacity, the taste, and the intelligence of the American individual whose choice finally determines the direction of American economic life.

First, as to capacity. A spate of literature has conjured up the fear that men may be reduced to robots, manipulated by psychological stimuli. Administrators of the great corporations do endeavor to intervene in private decision making through public relations work, propaganda, and advertising. The impression is created that a "mass man" has come into existence, conditioned to reflexes and capable of being manipulated. A little real science and a great deal of pseudo science supports this view.

Yet the evidence is not convincing, and it is increasingly less convincing as the level of prosperity, i.e., possible choice available to an individual, rises. Some studies made by Professor Harold Wolf and Dr. Lawrence Hinkle at the Cornell Medical School are impressive. They analyzed, using the best modern technique, the reactions of Hungarians who had been subjected for more than a decade to the most intense external conditioning processes. The conclusions did not bear out the proposition that men, by any presently known processes, can be deprived (save for the shortest periods of time and then only under conditions like those prevailing in a prison camp) of their inner capacity to determine their own values and to follow a course of conduct based on them. Incidental and temporary variations can be made; but the integrity of the human mind and the human heart cannot be controlled. (Taste presents a more difficult and complex problem. In some measure it can unquestionably be influenced, as most women choosing their fall clothes can testify.)

In deeper analysis the American economic republic just now

is suffering from growing pains. In the space of a generation, tens of millions of individuals have been admitted to and participate in a cultural life—for example, the life of universities—which formerly was closed save to a favored few. Not unnaturally this gives the impression that cultural standards are becoming diluted, even debased. Some reject culture outright; some decline it, finding that a good life exacts an unfamiliar measure of effort, study, and thinking. Some enter and remain at a low level; many go farther; their children go farther still. The top group is not declining. Proportionately it is growing. There is no reason to assume that the intellectual and cultural level of America will be permanently debased because great companies hire hucksters to advertise their wares. One must be indignant at the waste, but there is no occasion to despair. The greatest and most enlightened companies consciously seek to improve the level, or at least minimize the dangers, of their huckstering. In any case, the public in time arrives at a consensus, revolts, and insists on change—as it is beginning to do with the television operations at present.

Even wholesale misuse of mass media tends to right itself. Shortly after World War I a group of philanthropic New Yorkers, at the instance of the late Paul Warburg, surveying the output of radio (it was then perhaps as bad as television is today), decided to accumulate a fund so that once a week good music could be sent out over the radio as a public-spirited contribution. The writer was treasurer of that fund. In the course of a few months the fund began operation. But by that time the mere knowledge that the radio medium could be used to spread Beethoven as well as bawdy stories had compelled a change in radio habits. A generation later all America is habituated to symphonic music by mass media. Probably more Americans now hear classical music than all other listeners combined (though the Soviet audience we know little about). In economic effect, this powerfully affected several segments of industry, as any record dealer will testify.

The ultimate power which the individual thus has is the fact of his independent political existence. We have noted that abuse or failure by administrators of economic affairs provokes a political intervention. These repeated political interventions compel the American system of economic administration to comply with the public consensus. Our individual may no longer be able to determine affairs by his action or decision in respect of a farm or a forge or a small factory. But he can decide what he will consume, what he will do with his leisure, and what political issues interest him. He can control property locally by demanding zoning laws. He can require a maximum of veracity by outlawing false advertising. He can insist on a respectable measure of economic planning; he can accept, indeed he can demand, the social investment of capital (schools, universities, public services) which must accompany private investment if civilization is to be successful. In time he may even come to demand a civilization which is beautiful as well as productive. He has been doing all these things in the United States for more than a century, in steadily increasing degree.

In terms of industrial property, the system has unquestionably reduced most owners to a passive-receptive role. But in terms of choice of life and choice of political expression, the citizen of the American economic republic probably has as effective a means of control as individuals have ever achieved in a large country.

Thus our American economic republic begins to constitute itself. There are on the one hand the administrators of economic power. There is the State, through which action can be compelled. There is a public, increasingly capable of expressing a choice as to what it wants and capable of energizing political forces if the system does not provide it. The making of these choices follows lines which are neither purely political nor purely economic. They express the effective demand of individuals for a life they consider good. In reaching their conclusions in this respect, each looks for guidance in fields outside politics, outside advertising, and outside the board-rooms of corporations or government offices.

In result we seem to be moving toward a civilization in which economic organization is powerful in terms of physical acts of production and distribution, but whose power is severely limited in terms of determining wants. The system we have been describing can stimulate or vary wants somewhat. But at long last it must stand or fall by giving the citizens of the American economic republic what they actually do want, and not what administrators believe they ought to want. Though all the armies of Madison Avenue were arrayed against Columbia or Princeton or Leland Stanford, the future would lie with the campus spires.

It is easy, even fashionable, to be defeatist. We can say that men are merely products of suggestion, and that administrators of mass media at the behest of administrators of economic power groups do the suggesting. But there are always men who do not yield to suggestion. We can fear that men are prisoners of conformity. But there are always men who refuse to conform. We can fear that the honest, clear-thinking work of men who follow their minds and their hearts will not be as widely accepted as the pronouncements of courtiers of propaganda. But history is a steady record of the ultimate success of the men whose courage and integrity cannot be warped or corrupted. By comparative standards, we have a singularly effective system of civil rights and civil liberties, though its maintenance must be the constant preoccupation of every thinking American. We have yet to see the time in America when ideas do not eventually establish themselves to the extent merited by their validity.

This is the language of philosophy and not economics. Yet there is no other choice. As material prosperity grows, as individuals are no longer dominated chiefly by providing the animal necessities of existence, their range of choice increases.

Their choices are precisely the product of their philosophy. There is no man so humble he cannot within the four walls of his room, and confines of his own heart, make of his life as he wills, a warehouse, a palace, or a temple. There is no way of preventing men of mind and spirit who essay great adventures in science and social structure, in the humanities and esthetics, in poetry, in art, in the pure search for truth we call philosophy, from becoming architects of the lives of so many as well as of their own. There is no possibility in the American republic of preventing these individual choices and the architects, the counsellors, and the scholars who guide them from being the eventual determinants of the American economic system. Our individual, at long last, cannot escape contemplating life. The result of his contemplation will make of the economic republic what he wills.

V *A Long View of Peoples'*
Capitalism and Soviet Communism

The American economic system competes today for primacy with the Communist economic system devised in the Soviet Union. Because these systems are in conflict and because that conflict could become lethal, it is impossible to avoid asking certain questions. Are the systems so different that conflict is inevitable? If not, are they so different that they could not coexist? Since every force—demographic, economic, and technical—increasingly forces all parts of the world into involuntary contact, could there be cooperation between them in the economic task providing the world with adequate and acceptable economic base? Or must one of them overturn the other, as Communist doctrine proclaims and as much non-Communist thinking accepts?

SIMILARITY OF THE PROPERTY-
POWER DIMENSION

Both the Soviet and the American systems are, essentially, systems of power. The Soviet power system is, in theory and in practice, substantially complete. The American power system is only partial, but it embraces the major productive activities (aside from agriculture) of the American economy.

141

Surprisingly, both countries arrived at their power systems by approximately the same route.

Both the Soviet Union and the Western European area have evolved from a feudal matrix. In the feudal systems property meant relatively little; power derived through the State meant a great deal. In both areas power tended to crystallize into fragments. The boyar, or count, passed on his power position to his son. Increasingly he struggled to attach his power position to a particular patch of land. Title to property thus became increasingly important. Beginning in the late eighteenth century the industrial age emerged; with technical progress it exploded into expansion in the nineteenth. This brought new groups into the picture, men who could organize industrial enterprise.

In the United States, erosion of possessory property in industrial enterprises began in the mid-nineteenth century with the emergence of the corporation as enterprise owner. Corporations were, certainly, not then thought of as instruments of social change. In Czarist Russia, however, this process scarcely began. There, the industrialist was frequently a monopolist. He was also closely allied with the surviving institutions of the feudal State; and, in any event, some of the greatest economic functions in Czarist Russia were carried on by State organizations. When, as aftermath of the First World War, revolution swept Russia, evolution of the industrial property system was far less advanced than in the United States.

Precisely because in the United States the decline of personal-property relationship to industry came by evolution from the bottom (as stockholders multiplied, and as institutional holdings of stock substantially ended the personal relation of the man to the thing) and not by fiat from the top, the result was emergence of several hundred American power organizations: the great industrial corporations we have been considering. Unquestionably because in the Russian revolution the sweeping change was made by doctrinaire decision at the top, the Soviet result was a single Statist power structure. The principal organizational difference between the two systems lies exactly there. The American is pluralistic; the Soviet is, at least in appearance, monolithic. In America the State is not a total power system; the Soviet State claims complete power.

Yet a glance below the surface makes it clear that the American system is not as pluralistic as it appears—nor is the Soviet system as monolithic. There is no combination or group of great corporations in the United States planning, let alone plotting, the integrated use of their cooperative power. Communist propaganda persistently draws this picture, and possibly Soviet propagandists even believe it. But the fact, of course, is that such propaganda is merely a carry-over of pictures of mid-nineteenth century Russia and Europe. It is true that in America as elsewhere, men performing similar functions under more or less similar conditions, and dealing with similar problems, tend to think alike. But in America this has not meant uniform action by corporations and their managements, let alone planning. In any case the corporation manager of today is essentially a civil servant seeking reputation, power, and a pension; in most instances he has long since ceased to be an owner or a tycoon seeking billions. Obviously common attitudes do appear. There is common interest among corporation administrators in maintaining conditions permitting them to act with a minimum of control, and their enterprises to go on working; and there is a common desire for an orderly system in which they play a prominent part.

Specialists in the Soviet system tell us that the monolithic quality of Soviet economics is likewise open to question. Each department, state trust, or commissariat, and each of the component units within each department and commissariat struggle with other units to expand their function and their power. The ultimate struggle of each administrator is for an adequate share in the State budget which, for practical purposes, allocates functions (including his own), resources, material, and labor. Resistance of a small bureau against absorption into a larger one is motivated almost exactly as is the struggle of a small American corporation not to be absorbed by a larger one, or of a leading corporation to maintain its share of the market against some other giant who proposes to expand. Competition within the Soviet system is cast in the bureaucratic rather than in the commercial mold. Yet the stakes are much the same and the difference not too great. In the Soviet system there is a Statist power mechanism at the top which continually resolves these conflicts—frequently by methods which are anything but gentle. There is no recognized equivalent for this in the American system, save that, in extremes, the American State can intervene politically, as it has regularly done in every American economic crisis.

Even in social structure the differences are not as great as frequently supposed. Milovan Djilas' book, *The New Class,* demonstrated that a Communist government bureaucracy exercising economic power in various areas clings to its politically created and sanctioned offices and positions with a tenacity quite equal to that of corporation administrators seeking to hold their jobs and their power. Bureaucrats are, in effect, seeking to convert their power into a form of personal "property," just as the old feudal power holder sought to convert his Statist office into title to land. In doing so, the class structure evolving under Communism approximates some of the features of the structure evolving in the United States, and parallels some of the history of the late medieval period in Europe.

On the distributive side, of course, the results are different. But not too different. The theory is that the entire gross national product of the Soviet Union belongs to "the people," that is, the entire population of that State. It is distributed chiefly through the wage and salary system supplemented by old-age pensions and social security payments, more or less arbitrarily, in accordance with the central policies of the Soviet government. The system is not equalitarian in either country—nor, probably, should it be. Superior character, higher ability, greater capacity to render those services which society needs not only can but should be rewarded more highly. In any case the possessors of these qualities are usually in a position to command higher reward either in community esteem, or in direct personal benefit, or both. A Communist government claims to distribute these in accordance with processes of reason, also chiefly through wages and salaries supplemented by pension and social security payments. The American industrial system claims to distribute them in accordance with the catch-and-toss of the market for personal talent. In most cases, however, the Russian bureaucracy and the American commercial enterprise are essentially looking for the same qualities. It is a fair question whether the arbitrariness and injustice of a bureaucratic—any bureaucratic—system are not greater than the accidents and irrationalities of the American market system.

If the similarity is great, the divergences are no less striking. The surprising fact is that the real differences are rarely alluded to.

The Soviet system is a planned system and glories in that fact, though plans can and do go awry as did the recent Five Year Plan which has just been scrapped and reorganized into the now current Khrushchev Seven Year Plan. The American system is in its greatest outlines unplanned—though there is far more planning in the United States than is commonly realized. If accurate description of the entire American economy were made, this would be apparent. The fiscal needs of the United States will always be an important, perhaps the most important, element in American economy. This is a Treasury planning function. Next under that comes the currency credit system dominated by the Federal Reserve Board. Below that are a series of uncoordinated regulatory agencies with greater or less power to plan: the Interstate Commerce Commission, the Maritime Commission, the Civil Aviation Board, the Inter-state Oil Compact (and below it, coordinated State regula-tions), the Federal Power Commission, the Federal Commu-nications Commission, the Atomic Energy Commission, the Defense Department powers with respect to stockpiles of raw materials, and the vast system of agricultural controls cover-ing most major products from corn to peanuts. Once aggre-gated and coordinated, it would appear the outlines of the American planning system are already present and in opera-tion. No serious attempt has yet been made to coordinate these into any steady, defined national policy, save occasionally when depressions threaten.

On the distributive side, there are also major differences. The United States, as noted, is based on a (chiefly) non-Statist system of economic power; the Soviet Union on a Statist system depending from political power. To be excluded from the distribution system of economic power in the United States means that you are out of a job; and unemployment, even when accompanied by unemployment benefits, is an evil con-dition for any man. To be excluded from the political-economic power system in the Soviet Union means that you are in dis-grace—subsistence is usually in a prison camp, which is still worse. It is not wholly accidental that, throughout the entire history of the Soviet Union there have been, as a rule, more Soviet citizens in concentration camps than there have been unemployed in the United States. But whereas in the United States unemployment is regarded as a misfortune about which something can and must be done, the Soviet system until re-cently considered it quite normal and acceptable to have sev-eral millions live and die in varying degrees of misery behind barbed wire. One of Nikita Khrushchev's solid claims to esteem is that he has attempted to reduce the concentration camp population of his country.

Data are not available to the writer making possible a judg-ment as to over-all distribution of national income within the American and Soviet population groups, respectively. Obviously the American standard of living is over-all far higher than the Soviet. The lowest paid elements in it are entitled to an improvement in position. Most Soviet citizens are entitled to improvement in their position. Of interest is the fact that in both systems distribution especially in lower income groups is at long last matter of status, not of property. The American draws his unemployment benefits and eventually his old age pension, private, public, or both. The Soviet employee at the bottom draws his government pay, and also, eventually, an old age pension. The Soviet system claims to be all-inclusive, so that no one is left out. There are areas in the American system still uncovered.

It is permissible to hazard the guess that the two systems, while they differ, are not so different in their economic organization that, merely by reason of these organizational or purely economic differences, they must fight each other to the death. Neither, as far as one can see, is entitled to take the doctrinaire position that the other must perish if it is to be safe. If conflict must come about, its inevitability does not lie in the organizational or economic imperatives of either system. Conflict will come, more probably, from insistence by one or the other side that it must impose its domination or its philosophical outlook on the other.

FORMATION OF CAPITAL: LIKENESS AND DIFFERENCE

In America, formation of capital is essentially a function of the price-profit system. Private corporate enterprises, especially the great and dominant enterprises, make profits when they sell their product. From these profits they deduct an arbitrary portion called "depreciation." About half of the remaining profit (after such deduction) is not distributed to shareholders but is retained. In combination, the depreciation allowance plus profits account for three-fifths of American industrial capital formation.

These are, in a sense, forced savings. It is as though to the price there were added a sales tax whose proceeds were ticketed for capital expansion of the corporation. The company has, to be sure, a legal right to distribute all its profits instead of only a part, but the right is apparent rather than real. The economic imperative of the American corporation is that it shall continue to grow, certainly as long as there is demand for its product—and even if there is not, to find new areas in which it can produce and sell.

The Soviet system likewise arbitrarily conscripts capital. It schedules production and rations consumption. To a considerable extent, it uses the price system as well as a rationing system to scale down consumption in some lines and increase it in others. But the process is planned along doctrinaire lines of policy. The product and productivity not made available for consumption are directed by the Soviet State toward capital construction and development of its planning and choosing.

Here again the surprising fact is less the differences than the similarity in the two processes. In both cases, a power pyramid sets the price. In both cases, the result is an accumulation of surplus over cost, taken from consumers. In both cases the power pyramid determines the application of the resulting capital. In neither case is the public consulted. The American business concern will, of course, apply capital—that is, build plants, develop markets, and so forth—where it believes there is public demand. But in substantial measure the Soviet State must do the same thing—that is, must develop productivity and products, which it believes its people need or desire. Being a dictatorship, it is, naturally, far less immediately sensitive to needs and desires.

The Soviet State has not, however, yet faced the main problem. Where standards of living are low, decisions as to needs and desires are relatively easy to make. There is little doubt that a hungry population will want more food, or that an ill-housed population will need more shelter. Any move in any direction at this stage is a move toward what the subjects of a Communist State unquestionably want. Later, when productivity becomes high, the element of choice enters in. Then the public may want better housing more than it wants more automobiles, or vice versa. At this point determination (other than by consumers' demand) assumes a different dimension. It is one thing to give a public what it wants. It is another to give it what an all-wise State thinks it *ought* to want—which may be quite different and is far more difficult. As the Soviet Union increases its productivity, as it approximates the American level, it will encounter increasing difficulty in dictating application of capital without some means of ascertaining the desires of its people—though the Soviet rulers are far from having this problem at the moment.

From here out, difference between the two systems becomes more marked. It really is a philosophical difference. Does a benevolent dictatorship do better by its people than a system which allows the public to make its own choice and mistakes, and acquire its own experience? That problem has been argued through the ages. Any individual will have his own views; most Americans would never accept dictatorship however benevolent save in a very few fields of human activity. The Soviet Union, for example, steers a part of its productivity into the making and distribution of books, with the result that a book in the Soviet Union can be bought at one-fifth (or less) of the price of an equivalent book in the United States. This, some of us would think, is a solid advantage. But it would be hard to say that the value of an immense supply of inexpensive literature outweighs the fact that most of the Soviet city population must live three or more in a room. The excess productivity conscripted as capital, conceivably, might better be applied to more housing or cheaper clothing. Again, the Soviet Union will arbitrarily apply a substantial amount of excess production to widespread artistic activities. Even minor Russian cities have one or two theatres, concert halls, or opera companies performing at all times. Most American cities have to put up with a string of motion-picture theatres and an occasional road company on tour—though a good many of them have local symphony orchestras. Is the arbitrary decision more useful, everything considered, than the free choice decision?

Obviously the United States is here facing a problem peculiar to its own type of organization. The American problem is technical as well as philosophical and cultural. The productive system of the United States motivated by the pursuit of profit is, clearly, capable of producing all the tobacco, perfume, cigars, houses, and so on, that can be properly consumed. It is also capable, in addition, of producing enough to maintain (without sacrificing or seriously limiting anything else) subsidized books, theatres, opera, music, and painting. The Communist system can, arbitrarily, place its capital and its productivity where it wants them (minimum needs and wants having first been supplied). The United States does not have accepted and recognized techniques for doing this. Available to it are, of course, the standard methods of taxation and State subsidies, the annual grist of beneficences (private donations and gifts from benevolent and educational foundations). But the American prefers separation of many of these activities from State administration, partly because he holds a very dim view (not wholly unjustified) of the capacity of the American State to perform these functions well. Private beneficence, on the other hand, is both limited in scope and unpredictable.

We shall not know whether the Soviet system is really workable until its productive level rises to the point where there is available to the Soviet people a wide choice in consumption and, by consequence, choice of the kind of life each individual wishes to lead. My own feeling is that the Communist State, as it increases its per capita production, will be forced to give continuously greater weight to the desires and choices of its people in direct proportion to the growth of its productivity. Poverty dictates decisions; wealth increases the possibility, function, and appetite for choice. Ten men in a boat cast away at sea are socialist by hypothesis. They adopt a plan, ration what they have, carry out an iron system of controls. Each of those same ten men on a well-furnished and well-stored yacht in normal travel will follow his own tastes and desires. The authority of the officer of the castaway boat will be accepted because necessity imposes acceptance. The captain of the well-furnished yacht, endeavoring to exercise similar authority, would find, quite simply, that no one paid any attention to him.

In capital gathering the American system is better since the taking is painless, is acquiesced in, and provides comfortably for future development, while the Soviet system is obviously carried out by compulsion. Greater productivity should make it possible to mitigate, conceivably even limit the extent of, compulsion, provided (it is an enormous proviso to be sure) that the men holding compulsive power are willing to surrender it. Surrender of power under any power system is not usual; commonly, such surrender has to be compelled.

Within the commercial field the American pluralist system obviously permits far greater flexibility in application of capital than does the Communist system in the Soviet Union. If one corporation thinks it unnecessary to develop magnesium or titanium, another corporation, thinking differently, will be willing to enter the field, apply capital, and commence production. On the other hand, as noted, the American system is inflexible when it comes to applying capital outside the commercial field. It is a Herculean job to get the American State or its local subdivisions to deal adequately with hospitals, medicine, education, art, music, low-rent housing, urban development, and other noncommercial activities.

Here is real cause for American concern. Increasingly, both the level and the direction of consumption turn on the cultural capacity of the individual. Increasingly also, proper functioning of the economic as well as the political republic turns on the quality of tasks done *outside* our commercial or profit system: education, research, esthetic evolution. Increasingly, therefore, it will be necessary for Americans to find new ways of collecting or applying capital in those areas not within the fields occupied and operated by the profit system.

INTERNATIONAL ECONOMICS: COOPERATION OR CONFLICT?

The Rockefeller Brothers Fund report on international economics (*Foreign Economic Policy for the Twentieth Century*, Special Studies Project Report III, June 16, 1958, Rockefeller Brothers Fund) made one fact plain. Growing pressure of population and demand of all populations for an adequate standard of living will compel a wider base for any economic republic than can now be comprehended within the national borders of any existing State. This implies one of two things. Either the world will be divided into two zones, Communist and free, each attempting self-sufficiency, or a break will have to be found in the current impasse between the two. Such a break could be accomplished by conquest—but this means war, with destruction so great that either system, conquering or conquered, would have to begin over again. The alternative would be finding some avenue of cooperation. Neither side will—probably neither side can—abandon its major philosophical premises. Without doing so, can they accommodate to each other sufficiently to work together in major tasks?

The record of past efforts to accommodate has been bleak indeed. Yet there seems to be no essential reason why it cannot be done, provided cooperation is real and not an attempt by either to weaken the other, awaiting the moment of ultimate conflict. This observation, of course, applies to economic endeavor only. Common arrangements should be possible to supply underdeveloped areas with products, machinery, and techniques which they need, accompanied by a common understanding that they will share the benefits available to everyone concerned from the enhanced production thus engendered. Cooperation in such measures is theoretically entirely possible. American commercial power groups working with their government are quite as capable of accommodating to such arrangements as are the Soviet State production pyramids. This is about all that can be said now. Only the future will tell whether Soviet dogmatists will continue to insist that they and their system are unbearably threatened until they conquer the world by revolution, and maintain their conquests with tanks and rockets.

THE CONTROL OF POWER

Under the American system pyramids of corporate organization result in power. This power is actually controlled, as we have seen, by the operation of the public consensus which can engender public opinion leading to political intervention in any one of a number of forms. In this respect, the American economic system remains true (in broad lines) to the conception of the American democratic State.

So far as we are aware, there is no equivalent control element in respect of the pyramids of power set up by the Soviet government. That system must, of course, cope with the fact that its economic operations must work. They must not break down; they must not reach a point at which wholesale rebellion oversets the system; they must, to some extent, take account of the desires of their people. This is merely to say that they must not push their policies and methods to a point which destroys the minimum of acquiescence which any regime must have to survive. On the other hand, part of the strength and attractiveness of the Soviet system—attractiveness particularly to poverty-stricken countries which demand rapid evolution— is its capacity to move *against* the existing immediate desires of great masses of population while promising greater fulfill- ment at some later date. It can, for example, conscript great blocks of labor and use that labor as capital—a method not permitted (and happily unnecessary) in the American system. It can (up to a point) allocate the capital it forms to heavy goods in the teeth of popular desire for consumer goods, or to intangibles like technical education in face of widespread need for housing. It can do this by combining compulsion with the hope that future generations will be better off—the Com- munist substitute for the hope of heaven hereafter.

This is probably as much Russian as systemic. Never in Russian history has there been a government really responsive to population desires. The idea of "public consensus" is not wholly foreign to Russian thinking, but, save in local matters, it certainly has been foreign to effective Russian political practice, Czarist or Communist.

On the other hand, the Soviet system does establish its own variety of oligarchic controls, exercised chiefly through the machinery of the Communist Party. Theoretically, thinking among a tiny group of top Party committees and experts is continuous. The crises of Russian planning, which occurred after Stalin's death in April 1953 and again in the autumn of 1956, have been recently described by Fritz Schenk, a German Communist refugee, member of the East German Planning Commission ("Politics and Planning in the Soviet Empire,"

New Leader, January 5 and 12, 1950). Crises in the Soviet system likewise engender a form of political intervention though the means is that of intragovernment discussion, agitation, sometimes conspiracy, in the upper reaches of the Soviet dictatorship. Having no public to which appeal can be made and from which decision can be had, Party and planning committees, if they are unable to agree, can only have recourse to intrigue or other means by which one faction seeks power sufficient to impose its view over another. This appears to be the reason for the recurrent phenomenon of plots within or perhaps against the Soviet State (top executives or groups seeking to carry on conflicting policies and seeking to defend themselves), and for the ultradefensive countermeasures which have often included imprisonment and execution. The violences of these have recently shown some signs of amelioration.

Objections to the American system of "public consensus," which through public opinion checks or guides economic power, are those urged against all democratic systems. Its operations move slowly, sometimes erratically. Inequities go too long uncorrected. In company matters, technical information is not easily available or well understood. Swift changes of policy are not possible. On the other hand, the American public consensus invariably moves and engenders action along the lines of public acceptability. This makes for a more or less stable organizational situation. It also makes for continuous study and agitation in respect of unacceptable situations. In point of fact, if one takes a period of forty years (1919-1959), American progress toward social justice has been remarkable. No current means of comparing this with Soviet social progress is available. Clearly American thinking, now preoccupied with individual as well as mass social justice, has moved into an area which the statistically thinking Communists (who place a low valuation on individuality anyhow) have only barely sighted. Up to the present, their social as well

as individual justice has been a servant of the "revolution"—
that is to say, of the government—and not a servant of individual life.

One can only speculate. Assuming continued peace, in any
long view the American and Soviet systems would seem to be
converging rather than diverging so far as their organizational and many of their economic aspects are concerned. On
the other hand, nothing has yet occurred suggesting any
convergence of their philosophical objectives. To an American,
his economic system is means to an end—that end is individual
life. As yet, so far as appears, most Communists regard their
economic system as an end in itself, from which, when fully
realized, unspecified blessings will flow. One suspects that,
sooner or later, Russians will emerge demanding that the blessings actually shall flow to individuals. Evidence is not wanting
that the individual Russian heart is quite as warm as the
American.

Nineteenth and early twentieth century economic and social
thinking was concentrated on the subject of systems. These
were considered the chief determinants of life. A free market,
private property, individualist system—or a socialist system
as you chose—was the road to heaven; its opposite, an uneasy
descent into hell. An uncontrolled economic system promoted
initiative, developed strong men, was the basis of political
democracy. In opposite view, it enthroned property, exploited
men through wage-slavery, was the enemy of the good life
and good State. Socialism, its friends insisted, by eliminating
the profit motive, recognized society's debt to the weak as well
as to the strong, and protected the masses from exploitation.
Or, perhaps, it enthroned powerholders, forging the fetters
of a new serfdom. So ran the debate.

Current scholarship looks within each system, considering its
internal content and results more important than its outward
doctrine or form. By that analysis socialist economic systems

may also be, or may become, politically democratic, offering higher content of individualist development than some forms of capitalism. Politically democratic capitalist systems adhering to private-property profit-motive doctrines may also be frameworks for collectivist power pyramids, and these may combine the advantages of planning with the values of individual choice. Students have begun to analyze the phenomena of organization which emerge within each system, evaluating each by its end product in human development.

Increasingly we are coming to learn that human content is the real basis on which economic and social systems must be judged. As socialism and modern American capitalism are led by their evolution to converge in certain aspects, the human results of the two systems emerge as the criteria of judgment. American experience appears to show that the power pyramids we call "corporations," despite their size, can be checked by public consensus and disciplined by political intervention. Conceivably, the evolving Communist system may also in time accept creation through freedom of expression and thought of a public consensus affording political correctives for abuse of Statist power.

America has prevented monopoly of property, considering it inimical to the full development of human beings. But she has accepted large-scale collective industrial organizations which reflect themselves in power. Having limited the possibilities of abuse based on property, she is gradually but effectively restraining power. On the other hand, she is barely beginning to explore the possibilities of planning. In the younger Russian experiment, based on unparalleled monopoly of power, the Soviet Union is working out the added potentials derived from planning, which that power makes possible. As yet, she hardly apprehends the possibility that the power itself can and must be kept in bounds, and that it can be used without destroying the men it is supposed to serve.

Struggle between the two systems arises, not because of

their structural incompatibility, but because their respective operators differ in their fundamental conceptions of the significance of men and the importance of men's free choice of life. At the economic level, twentieth-century productivity is rapidly making such free choice attainable. The price appears to be concentration of economic power. Almost inevitably, in the end, all societies will demand organization of power sufficient to realize the economic potential. The issue is whether they will also demand restraint and guidance of that power sufficient to permit the self-determination of men.

On the solution of that problem hangs the fate of each people as each faces its evolving social-economic system. More yet: on it hangs the capacity of peoples to prevent their systems from making war (in any of its overt or covert forms) on other systems or peoples. Hope of survival as well as quest for Utopia are thus bound in resolving the issue of economic power in twentieth-century society.

Notes to Chapter I

1. *Formation of capital*

The original study of capital formation (1919-1947), whose figures are used in this chapter, was a private exploration made by the writer for Mr. (now Governor) Nelson A. Rockefeller, who has long been interested in the subject. Dr. Irvin Bussing, then Consulting Economist for the Savings Banks Trust Company, made the calculations. He considered them rough; further scholarly analysis might vary them somewhat. Both he and the writer (associated with him in that study) were convinced that further refinement, however, would not substantially change the picture. The authoritative study subsequently made by the Office of Business Economics of the United States Department of Commerce, published in its *Survey of Current Business* (cited in the text), has confirmed the pattern of our early estimates. The decade 1947-1956 emphasized that, so far as industry was concerned, retained profits plus depreciation constitute the preponderant source of American industrial capital. Partial figures for 1958 follow the same pattern. Mild depression apparently does not greatly change the outline. Outside the public utility field, a business enterprise which has "come of age," now, is one which can satisfy the bulk of its capital needs from internal sources.

For working purposes, it may be taken that 60 per cent of all industrial capital is thus internally generated.

2. *The rôle of bank credit*

Aside from wartime distortions, bank credit appears to

account for approximately 20 per cent of incoming industrial capital funds. Whether this is good banking or not the writer is in doubt. Theoretically, bank credit should be reserved for goods in process, and moving toward ultimate destination, that is, to consumption or final use. That rule has apparently never been strictly adhered to in American finance. Of more interest in our study is the fact that bank credit is chiefly available to corporations which can anticipate internal generation of capital; probably much of it represents an anticipation through bank loans of funds to be generated in course of the borrowers' business which will be used to pay off the bank loans.

3. *The rôle of the "institutional investor"*

There is ample room for discussion as to which among the groups of institutional investors is of greatest importance in determining the *locus* of economic power. The life insurance companies are far and away the largest investors of capital. But, by law, their capacity to invest in equities and common stock is severely limited—so far as the writer is aware, the maximum amount of such investments allowed is 5 per cent of assets, and in many states less. Few insurance companies buy common stocks up to the maximum limit allowed them. The total assets of life insurance companies—somewhat more than $100 billion—would at maximum permit them only to invest in slightly more than $5 billion of common stock. This they have not done.

Insurance companies commonly double their assets in each decade, in geometric progression. Ten years from now, they might be in a position to invest $10 billion (their total assets would then be perhaps $200 billion). A decade after that, when their assets will probably be $400 billion, their total common stock investment capacity might be $20 billion.

But they are obviously not exercising this power at present. For instance, the *Wall Street Journal* for Tuesday, December 9, 1958, reported that thirty-three major life insurance companies had invested in common stocks during the first forty-eight weeks of 1958, a total of $148.5 million—or 1.3 per cent of their total investments for that period.

Pension trusts on the other hand are growing with great rapidity, and they are increasingly pressed to find common stock investments. Professor Paul Howell, writing in the *Harvard Business Review* for November-December 1958, asserted that their goal should be a far greater investment in equities and correspondingly less in bonds. A proportion of 50 per cent in common stocks as desirable is frequently mentioned among professional managers of such funds. This would give a present investing capacity of up to $15 billion in common stock *now* (though the actual investment has been considerably less—possibly in the neighborhood of $8 billion). But the pension trusts are growing with great rapidity; also they are increasingly using (and are under pressure to use) their capacity to purchase common stocks. They are already in a position, by joint action, to acquire control of a number of corporations having industrial leadership.

4. *Mutual funds*

The third candidate for institutional power is the group of institutions known as "mutual funds." There are approximately 150 of these in varying degree of size, though a majority are relatively small. Their aggregate assets are in the neighborhood of $13 billion at date of writing—almost entirely invested in common stocks. Unlike pension trusts, however, there is no certainty that they will continue to grow. In most mutual funds, the small stockholder at any time may demand that he be paid the market value (less charges) of his proportionate share of the fund portfolio. If at any time more individuals wish to liquidate their holdings than wish to buy into mutual funds, these funds would be compelled to sell their stocks in the open market. Maintenance of their present position and their increase in size, therefore, depends on the continued popularity of this form of personal investment. Based on the present situation, they are likely to continue to grow. But it would seem likely that the pension trusts, which not only can but must grow and which cannot be put under great pressure to sell, will eventually be the most important institutional group.

5. *The relative absorption of common stocks by institutions*

If the total volume of common stock of American enterprises were increasing in exact proportion to purchase of such stock by insurance companies, pension trusts, and mutual funds, there would be no shift in the *locus* of power over corporate structure. But in fact the increase of common stock is relatively not great. Further, the few hundred established leaders which control the bulk of American industry have not been seeking additional capital through issue of new common stock. They have, as noted, relied on their internal generation of capital, plus a certain amount of increase in bonded debt. In respect of bonds, of course, their interest payment is deductible from income, giving a tax advantage. Though there are occasional common stock increases among the corporate leaders (both Standard Oil of New Jersey and General Motors have floated additional common stock issues), the bulk of such issues has taken place in the public utilities companies; this is because public utilities have more difficulty in generating internal capital owing to rate regulation.

Pension trusts, insurance companies, and, in large measure, the mutual funds when they buy stocks primarily seek the stocks of the established companies precisely because they are established, and therefore are well-seasoned investments. Until some change occurs, accumulation of institutional stock buying in these companies almost necessarily will continue to exceed the issue of new stock by such companies. As this progresses, the *locus* of economic power gravitates toward the institutions.

Obviously, investment in common stocks and established corporations by institutions does not mean that capital is thereby supplied to such corporations. The institutions are buying from Nym stock which he bought from Bardolph, who in turn bought it from Pistol, who in turn bought it from Sir John Falstaff, who inherited it from his father, who founded the business. Presumably Nym will reinvest the price he receives in something else—possibly in a large life insurance policy or in shares of mutual funds or the like. For our purposes, tracing the flow of such capital is not important and I have not attempted it. It is sufficient for this argument that the rapid growth of institutions and their increased purchases of common stock increasingly accumulates in a few institutional administrators the historical voting power.

Notes to Chapter II

1. *Elimination of "ownership" or "proprietorship"*

There is no source for this proposition. As has been noted, this is not the old "separation of ownership from control" pointed out in *The Modern Corporation and Private Property* by the writer and Dr. Gardiner C. Means more than thirty-five years ago. This is something more profound—the increasing elimination of proprietary ownership itself, and its replacement by, substantially, a power system.

2. *The mechanics*

The best recent study of the vanishing position of the stockholder is contained in Joseph A. Livingston's *The American Stockholder* (Philadelphia, J. B. Lippincott & Co., 1958). Popular in form, this is also a scholarly contribution. He points out that out of some 3,000 companies whose stocks are traded on American stock exchanges, only twenty-four proxy contests occurred in 1956 and only twelve in 1957. Few of these concerned really powerful corporations; the fight over the New York Central in 1955 was an exception. It is of incidental interest to note that in that year 45 per cent of all of the stock in New York Central was registered in "brokers' names," that is, was in the hands of speculators and traders rather than investors who have some psychological commitment to the enterprise.

The technique of proxy contests is described in *Proxy Contests for Corporate Control*, by Edward Ross Aranow and

Herbert A. Einhorn (New York, Columbia University Press, 1957). This is strictly technical: the authors risk no social conclusions, as did Livingston. But one conclusion forces itself on any student. For practical purposes, the corporate system is not substantially affected by theoretical ability of stockholders to change management.

3. *The industrial result*

While the stockholder has been vanishing, probably by his own volition, into a growing statistical category of Americans, and while the number of Americans who have, through institutions, a stake in the value and dividends of stock has been growing to include many tens of millions of Americans, industry itself appears to have been steadily integrating. A literate history, for example, of growth of integration in the oil industry is contained in *Growth of Integrated Oil Companies* by Professors John G. McClain and Robert William Haigh of the Harvard Business School, published by the Division of Research, Graduate School of Business Administration, Harvard University, Cambridge, 1954. Similar histories would disclose like integration in a good many other industries. A somewhat different point of view is given in *Economic Concentration and the Monopoly Problem* by Dean Edward S. Mason (Cambridge, Harvard University Press, 1957). Dean Mason seems to consider the social question involved as the degree of permissible power gravitating toward corporations. He rightly observes that while big business has important consequences with the functioning of economy and society, the literature has not as yet related these consequences either to business size or to general concentration. He suggests that problems do exist but does not discuss them.

Discussion of the results nevertheless does continue in philosophical circles. Professor Marshall Dimock, in his book, *A Philosophy of Administration Toward Creative Growth* (New York, Harper & Brothers, 1958), analyzes the problems at length, making the flat statement that heads of big corporations (or big labor unions, or any aggregation of economic power) are engaged in governing (p. 62) with which the writer naturally agrees. He comes to the conclusion that the problem of vanishing ownership and its replacement by a power organism may well give rise to bureaucracy, and to the emergence of the bureaucratic state. This follows closely the line of the late Walton Hamilton's *The Politics of Industry* (New York, Alfred A. Knopf, 1957). Dimock would argue for a wide degree of deconcentration. Joseph A. Livingston (*op. cit.*) considers that the stockholders (*a fortiori,* holders of insurance policies, pension trust rights, or participators in mutual funds) are out of it. They have not much interest in anything except the dividends they receive. In any event they are in no position to act. *The Dynamics of American Economy,* by Charles H. Hession, S. M. Miller, and Curwen Stoddart (New York, Alfred A. Knopf, 1956) comes to the conclusion (p. 121) that the typical structure of the large corporation is a variety of social system with a definite dynamic. The writer would agree with this, disagreeing with the conclusions reached by Professor C. Wright Mills in *The Power Elite* (New York, Oxford University Press, 1956). Mills thinks the entire system is planless and formless, as large economic aggregations slowly absorb into themselves a mélange of business figures, military figures, and political personalities. The argument hardly stands up in view of the very solid achievements of the American system.

We have not in this chapter attempted to deal with many of these questions. What is clear is that the mass of Americans who have, directly or indirectly, a stake in receiving the fruits of the corporate process other than as wage earners or consumers is steadily growing. The six or seven millions of direct stockholdings (this is the rough estimate of the New York Stock Exchange) do not include the far greater number of millions of "indirect" stockholdings through the institutions. But as these indirect interests increase, direct and indirect stockholders as individuals cease to be a factor in the organization and direction of the great industrial pyramids. Such influence as they have is exercised politically; and they do have political influence, exercised through the democratic state. This is the present reality of "Peoples' Capitalism."

Communist society, in equivalent language, insists that the entire population is "owner" of the State resources. Members of that population also have very little to say about organization and direction—under Communist practice their political influence is reduced to that minimum which cannot be prevented or guided even by secret police, propaganda, and State-controlled information.

In both cases, it is clear that we are faced less with problems of economics than with problems of power.

Notes to Chapter III

1. *The theory of power*

At present there is none; the writer claims no competence to evolve one: he can merely point out its necessity. Marshall Dimock in *A Philosophy of Administration Toward Creative Growth* (New York, Harper & Brothers, 1958) fully apprehends the fact that organization, in current American dogma, implies power. He takes the view (p. 167) that there are two approaches to power, the mechanist and the creative. The former is brittle; the latter is "based on enterprise and co-operation at all levels. . . . Power without spirit is nothing. . . . Power without large numbers of growing individuals is already dead." Dimock, of course, did not set for himself the problem of attacking the whole question.

An interesting volume, *Authority,* edited by Professor Carl Friedrich of Harvard (Cambridge, Harvard University Press, 1958) collects a series of studies by a number of scholars. In general these scholars assume power of some sort as a fact; "authority" is power in right (legitimate) with justice (legitimately used). Bertrand de Jouvenel (in *Authority, op. cit.,* Chap. 10) thinks that authority and power are the same, drawing distinction between naked authority (brute power) and a "pure relation of authority" (B does the bidding of A simply because of A's prestige and accepted position). Of interest is de Jouvenel's savage comment (p. 164):

The individual whom I can see is institution-ridden and institution-supported. The whole social field is built over with structures of various natures, offering goods, services, positions, and posting up the conditions on which they will deliver these goods or confer these positions; and with no one of these structures can the individual haggle: it is not for him to discuss the conditions of his joining either the staff of General Motors or the Union of Automobile Workers. This is a universe of posted prices in the most general meaning of the word "price." And it is highly doubtful whether any other kind of social universe can exist.

Understanding of this is widespread, as such terms as "adjusting," "fitting-in" testify. The individual per se moves within this organized world, reaching the goal he has chosen insofar as he has taken the paths provided and satisfied the conditions. The individual cannot fight an organization unless he happens to be at the head of another organization (say, Walter Reuther), or unless he initiates a move among his fellows (say, John Hampden).

2. The General Philosophy of Power

I am indebted to George E. Gordon Catlin's excellent compendium, *The Story of the Political Philosophers* (New York, Tudor Publishing Company, 1947), for introduction to the relatively few theorists who have examined power (see Index), particularly for calling attention to Althusius (*op. cit.*, pp. 159 ff.). Catlin's essay, "Authority and Its Critics," in the cited volume, *Authority*, gives perhaps the best review of current thinking about power. Dr. Hannah Arendt in an article, "Authority in the Twentieth Century" (*Review of Politics*, Vol. 18, No. 4, October 1956), draws a line between legitimate and illegitimate power. She contends that authority has substantially disappeared in the twentieth-century world, that is, that there are no longer "valid legitimate principles of coercion" (in *Authority*, *op. cit.*, p. 88). The conclusion has a modicum of justification as one looks at the chaos of some parts of the international political world. But I do not think it valid as a generalization. Certainly it is not valid within the United States.

3. *The economic field*

So far as I know, examination of the philosophy of power as applied through economic organizations (corporations, labor unions, etc.) is unplowed ground. Nevertheless in the United States such power obviously does exist; obviously also it does not rest on naked capacity to coerce. Any corporation, and for that matter most labor unions, relying solely on such capacity would be out of business in relatively short order. I have here tried to relate "legitimate power" to function, and to erect the fact (it is a fact) of "public consensus" as the process by which the holding and use of economic power is legitimatized.

Bertrand Russell tackled the whole question twenty years ago (London, George Allen and Unwin, Ltd., *Power, A New Social Analysis*, 1938) and he rested part of his argument on the writer's, *The Modern Corporation and Private Property*. His conclusion, "Permanent political solution of the problem of power is cooperation, not domination" (Catlin, *op. cit.*, p. 58) is *par excellence* applicable to economic power.

The writer believes he is not hopelessly romantic in transferring into economic organization Catlin's conclusion as to power in the political field:

Primarily the fount of power is in the ideal, since it alone gives consistency. For the rest, let us recall that States are not maintained or changes made by words, but by disciplined action directed by ideas by which the world is ruled.

Notes to Chapter IV

1. *The Economic Republic*

The requirements for a modern economic republic are matter of personal opinion: they need little academic footnote. The possibilities inherent in existing fact are noted and brought together. The result differs from a Utopia primarily in that the requirements are related to current reality and, perhaps hopefully, are assumed to be in the realm of the possible. Actually, the attempt to think into existence an improved organization of our own time differs from construction of a Utopia only in the fact that the former is thought to be possible in a political generation; the latter assumes passage of many years before reality.

Creation of Utopias has historically been an avocation of close students of their own time. That subject is worth an essay in itself. Plato is the most famous and possibly the oldest architect of a Utopia: he wrote *The Republic,* and later, perhaps as a result, got his chance at practical politics. Unfortunately, his opportunity came as a member of Critias' government of the Thirty Tryants, one of the worst Athens had ever encountered. He left it in disgust. Perhaps a better chance was offered when as consultant he joined in drafting the constitution of the new city of Megalopolis, designed to become capital of the associated Greek City-States after their successful defense against the Persian invasion. Regrettably Megalopolis did not have a brilliant history. Plato's dream Republic nevertheless is an active influence today.

Other Utopians have fared similarly. St. Augustine and his "City of God" is sometimes cited in this connection, but I think he is outside the guild for the excellent reason that he insisted his kingdom was not and should not be of this world. In terms of continuing political impact perhaps he did the best job of any; but he did not attempt the task of direct political creation. Niccolo Machiavelli, in his time, was directly discussing immediate politics and really was campaigning. His claim to being a Utopian is thus slender, but can, I think, be adequately grounded on the closing chapter of *The Prince*— an impassioned plea for a united Italy. (Five hundred years later this dream was realized.)

Thomas More (later "Sir" and "Saint"), whose volume established the name "Utopia," has a more complicated history. Unquestionably he was daydreaming of an unreal future when he wrote it. Yet much of it is an astute critique of contemporary conditions. It cannot be dismissed merely as fantasy. The somewhat surprising result was that he became for a time favorite at the court of Henry VIII, had occasional chances to express his views in councils of state, but in the end fell foul of the religious upheaval and was beheaded. An astonishing number of ideas found in *The Utopia* are current in the thinking of today. I think he is more alive than his not quite contemporary critic and competitor, Sir Francis Bacon, who attempted to rewrite and improve on Sir Thomas More in the *New Atlantis*. Bacon was an abler courtier, an astuter politician, a deeper scholar, though in the writer's opinion far less of a man than More. In any case, I think he was not writing a new Utopia but was trying to improve More's project.

The history is far too long to discuss, despite its fascination. The list of Utopians include as diverse characters as Dr. Samuel Johnson (*Rasselas*) and H. G. Wells. None of them was completely divorcing his dream from a realistic base grounded on observation.

I am not, in this chapter, attempting to join that noble list of philosophers, writers, and dreamers. The attempt to set out some of the guide-lines of the economic republic here is intended to be realistic. By that I mean that I think the suggestions here made are quite likely to be matter of current political campaigning within the next five or six years (if not sooner) and that the social and political substructure for most of them is already in existence.

2. *Planning*

The word "planning" has fallen into the lingo of stereotyped political controversy: you are for it as a solution; you are against it as a danger. Analysis of what planning is seems to be absent.

Factually, planning is not panacea and cannot be: it is a process by which solutions can be reached, not a solution in itself. Planning does not remove conflicts of interest. Each economic sector will struggle to attain the most advantageous position it can, and will not be vividly interested in the problems or difficulties of other sectors. Plans when made may be successful, or they may be hopelessly inept or oppressive.

What the planning mechanism does do is to supply a means and a method by which these conflicts can be resolved. The data on which plans are constructed necessarily forces consideration and development of principles on which conflicts may be resolved, and of criteria by which solutions may be judged, revised, or improved. In economics we are slowly pounding out a sort of common law whereby conflicts of interest and moral claims of individuals may be resolved other than by brutal economic struggle. In this respect there is even a modicum of coincidence in thinking between non-Communist and Communist philosophers, though their solutions are usually different and their value systems are in many respects opposed. The area of agreement consists in a growing feeling on all sides that there must be an adequate degree of order, and that there must be a generally available social justice. Their disagreement lies in complete difference as to the relative claims of order and freedom, and substantial divergence on the bases of social justice.

Some of these differences may disappear as Communist countries draw more nearly even with the United States in terms of productivity. I believe this is more than wishful thinking.

This convergence does not in the writer's judgment go very far toward solving the age-old problem of will-to-conquer imperialism (real imperialism, not the Communist cliché that capitalism is imperialism by hypothesis). So far as the writer can discover, no mere likeness of economic systems has prevented ambitious politicians in one country (as in the case of the U.S.S.R. today) from yearning to take, hold and exercise power over the peoples of other countries. Throughout the eighteenth, nineteenth, and early twentieth centuries the Western European countries, which had the greatest similarity to each other, tore themselves and the world to pieces in a series of struggles.

Notes to Chapter V

A Long View of Peoples' Capitalism and Soviet Communism

The fact that socialist and capitalist industrial organization tend to converge in their organizational aspects is shocking to many American minds. Yet there is solid ground for believing that free societies may develop out of collectivist States and that free States may develop collectivist forms of economic organization. I can commend a recent and singularly thoughtful book discussing this possibility: *The Economy, Liberty and the State* by Professor Calvin B. Hoover (New York, Twentieth Century Fund, 1959), a first-rate American economist who has made six visits to the Soviet Union and has studied its economy with extreme care. I recommend particularly Chapter 12, "Economic Systems and Liberty: Analysis of the Record." It is important to note that the threat to liberty, in Calvin Hoover's view, comes not from the concentration of organization but from the union of that organization with the State. Russian Communism is the completeness of Statism. Yugoslav Communism, on the other hand, seeks to set up "a competitive, free market economy but with collective ownership instead of private ownership of the means of production—a sort of capitalism without individual stockholders" (*ibid.*, p. 413), with the State acting as a central planning organization but setting forth only general objectives in lines of development, implementing them by monetary, fiscal, and credit controls, and by control over investment (*ibid.*, p. 416).

". . . there would not have to be much further evolutionary development of corporations in the United States or much further redistribution of income before the difference between the so-called capitalistic systems and the so-called socialist systems of the Yugoslav type would lose their sharpness" (*ibid.*, pp. 423-24).

This is not to say that there will not be conflict between the Communist world and our own. But conflict will not be over economic formations of organization.

Index

Adams, Henry, 73
Advertising, 82, 136-37, 138
Age of Innocence, The (Wharton), 73
Agriculture, 94, 128, 129-30, 146; Department of, 128, 130
Ahab, King, 14
Air transport, 126, 128, 130
Aldrich, Nelson, 125
Allied Chemical Corporation, 4
Althaus, Johan (Althusius), 79, 169
Aluminum Company of America, 4, 71, 107
American Capitalism: A System of Countervailing Power (Galbraith), 19
American Stockholder, The (Livingston), 105, 164
American Telephone and Telegraph Company, 4, 16, 35-36, 45-46, 63, 92-97 *passim*, 102
America's Needs and Resources (Dewhurst), 120
Anaconda Copper Company, 15
Antitrust regulation, 84-85, 103-4, 127. *See also* Monopoly
"Apologetics of 'Managerialism'" (Mason), 117
Aranow, Edward Ross, 164
Arendt, Dr. Hannah, 169
Armour Institute, 37
Armstrong investigation, 10
Atomic energy, 95, 126; Act, 126; Commission, 56, 130, 146
Augustine, St., 172
Authority (Friedrich, ed.), 168, 169
"Authority," and power, 168-69

"Authority and Its Critics" (Catlin), 169
"Authority in the Twentieth Century" (Arendt), 169

Bacon, Sir Francis, 172
Ballinger-Pinchot investigation, 14
Banks: as capital source, 31-35, 37, 39-41, 159-60; as pension trustees, 50-51, 55; regulation, 93, 125; farm loan, 129. *See also* Federal Reserve; Fiduciaries
Baruch, Bernard, 73
Basing-point system, 84-85
Belmont, August, 4
Bentham, Jeremy, 96
Berle, Adolf A., Sr., 2
Big business, 3-15 *passim*, 62, 165-66
Bonds, 31, 34, 35, 36, 37; private placement, 44; vs. common stocks, 162
Brandeis, Louis D., 2, 11, 13-14, 124
British Broadcasting Corporation, 97
Bureau of Mines, 128, 129
Bureaucracy, 62, 143-45, 166
Business: liberals' stereotypes, 11-12; size and concentration, social questions, 13-14, 62, 165-66; obligations of economic statesmanship, 15; private vs. government, 15 (*see also* Government)
Business Economics, office of, 128, 159
Businessmen: preface for, 3-10; recognition and prestige, 4-8; in

177